T0336494

THIS IS YOUR **PASSBOOK**® FOR ...

MAINTENANCE AND CONSTRUCTION HELPER

NATIONAL LEARNING CORPORATION®
passbooks.com

Copyright © 2018 by

NLC®

National Learning Corporation

212 Michael Drive, Syosset, NY 11791
(516) 921-8888 • www.passbooks.com
E-mail: info@passbooks.com

PUBLISHED IN THE UNITED STATES OF AMERICA

PASSBOOK® SERIES

THE *PASSBOOK® SERIES* has been created to prepare applicants and candidates for the ultimate academic battlefield – the examination room.

At some time in our lives, each and every one of us may be required to take an examination – for validation, matriculation, admission, qualification, registration, certification, or licensure.

Based on the assumption that every applicant or candidate has met the basic formal educational standards, has taken the required number of courses, and read the necessary texts, the *PASSBOOK® SERIES* furnishes the one special preparation which may assure passing with confidence, instead of failing with insecurity. Examination questions – together with answers – are furnished as the basic vehicle for study so that the mysteries of the examination and its compounding difficulties may be eliminated or diminished by a sure method.

This book is meant to help you pass your examination provided that you qualify and are serious in your objective.

The entire field is reviewed through the huge store of content information which is succinctly presented through a provocative and challenging approach – the question-and-answer method.

A climate of success is established by furnishing the correct answers at the end of each test.

You soon learn to recognize types of questions, forms of questions, and patterns of questioning. You may even begin to anticipate expected outcomes.

You perceive that many questions are repeated or adapted so that you can gain acute insights, which may enable you to score many sure points.

You learn how to confront new questions, or types of questions, and to attack them confidently and work out the correct answers.

You note objectives and emphases, and recognize pitfalls and dangers, so that you may make positive educational adjustments.

Moreover, you are kept fully informed in relation to new concepts, methods, practices, and directions in the field.

You discover that you arre actually taking the examination all the time: you are preparing for the examination by "taking" an examination, not by reading extraneous and/or supererogatory textbooks.

In short, this PASSBOOK®, used directedly, should be an important factor in helping you to pass your test.

MAINTENANCE & CONSTRUCTION HELPER

DUTIES

A Maintenance and Construction Helper does a variety of semiskilled manual tasks in construction, maintenance and repair activities.

SCOPE OFTHE EXAMINATION

The written test will consist entirely of a multiple-choice written test in which candidates may be examined for a knowledge of: basic hand and small power tools and their uses; operating characteristics and minor maintenance requirements of small gasoline engines and various types of small power equipment; various construction materials and their uses; basic arithmetic; rulers and tape measures within a 1 /16th of an inch; safety practices and procedures; applicable vehicle codes; interpersonal skills; the ability to read and understand simple safety signs and work orders; and other necessary knowledge, skills, and abilities.

———

HOW TO TAKE A TEST

I. YOU MUST PASS AN EXAMINATION

A. WHAT EVERY CANDIDATE SHOULD KNOW

Examination applicants often ask us for help in preparing for the written test. What can I study in advance? What kinds of questions will be asked? How will the test be given? How will the papers be graded?

As an applicant for a civil service examination, you may be wondering about some of these things. Our purpose here is to suggest effective methods of advance study and to describe civil service examinations.

Your chances for success on this examination can be increased if you know how to prepare. Those "pre-examination jitters" can be reduced if you know what to expect. You can even experience an adventure in good citizenship if you know why civil service exams are given.

B. WHY ARE CIVIL SERVICE EXAMINATIONS GIVEN?

Civil service examinations are important to you in two ways. As a citizen, you want public jobs filled by employees who know how to do their work. As a job seeker, you want a fair chance to compete for that job on an equal footing with other candidates. The best-known means of accomplishing this two-fold goal is the competitive examination.

Exams are widely publicized throughout the nation. They may be administered for jobs in federal, state, city, municipal, town or village governments or agencies.

Any citizen may apply, with some limitations, such as the age or residence of applicants. Your experience and education may be reviewed to see whether you meet the requirements for the particular examination. When these requirements exist, they are reasonable and applied consistently to all applicants. Thus, a competitive examination may cause you some uneasiness now, but it is your privilege and safeguard.

C. HOW ARE CIVIL SERVICE EXAMS DEVELOPED?

Examinations are carefully written by trained technicians who are specialists in the field known as "psychological measurement," in consultation with recognized authorities in the field of work that the test will cover. These experts recommend the subject matter areas or skills to be tested; only those knowledges or skills important to your success on the job are included. The most reliable books and source materials available are used as references. Together, the experts and technicians judge the difficulty level of the questions.

Test technicians know how to phrase questions so that the problem is clearly stated. Their ethics do not permit "trick" or "catch" questions. Questions may have been tried out on sample groups, or subjected to statistical analysis, to determine their usefulness.

Written tests are often used in combination with performance tests, ratings of training and experience, and oral interviews. All of these measures combine to form the best-known means of finding the right person for the right job.

II. HOW TO PASS THE WRITTEN TEST

A. *NATURE OF THE EXAMINATION*

To prepare intelligently for civil service examinations, you should know how they differ from school examinations you have taken. In school you were assigned certain definite pages to read or subjects to cover. The examination questions were quite detailed and usually emphasized memory. Civil service exams, on the other hand, try to discover your present ability to perform the duties of a position, plus your potentiality to learn these duties. In other words, a civil service exam attempts to predict how successful you will be. Questions cover such a broad area that they cannot be as minute and detailed as school exam questions.

In the public service similar kinds of work, or positions, are grouped together in one "class." This process is known as *position-classification*. All the positions in a class are paid according to the salary range for that class. One class title covers all of these positions, and they are all tested by the same examination.

B. *FOUR BASIC STEPS*

1) Study the announcement

How, then, can you know what subjects to study? Our best answer is: "Learn as much as possible about the class of positions for which you've applied." The exam will test the knowledge, skills and abilities needed to do the work.

Your most valuable source of information about the position you want is the official exam announcement. This announcement lists the training and experience qualifications. Check these standards and apply only if you come reasonably close to meeting them.

The brief description of the position in the examination announcement offers some clues to the subjects which will be tested. Think about the job itself. Review the duties in your mind. Can you perform them, or are there some in which you are rusty? Fill in the blank spots in your preparation.

Many jurisdictions preview the written test in the exam announcement by including a section called "Knowledge and Abilities Required," "Scope of the Examination," or some similar heading. Here you will find out specifically what fields will be tested.

2) Review your own background

Once you learn in general what the position is all about, and what you need to know to do the work, ask yourself which subjects you already know fairly well and which need improvement. You may wonder whether to concentrate on improving your strong areas or on building some background in your fields of weakness. When the announcement has specified "some knowledge" or "considerable knowledge," or has used adjectives like "beginning principles of…" or "advanced … methods," you can get a clue as to the number and difficulty of questions to be asked in any given field. More questions, and hence broader coverage, would be included for those subjects which are more important in the work. Now weigh your strengths and weaknesses against the job requirements and prepare accordingly.

3) **Determine the level of the position**

Another way to tell how intensively you should prepare is to understand the level of the job for which you are applying. Is it the entering level? In other words, is this the position in which beginners in a field of work are hired? Or is it an intermediate or advanced level? Sometimes this is indicated by such words as "Junior" or "Senior" in the class title. Other jurisdictions use Roman numerals to designate the level – Clerk I, Clerk II, for example. The word "Supervisor" sometimes appears in the title. If the level is not indicated by the title, check the description of duties. Will you be working under very close supervision, or will you have responsibility for independent decisions in this work?

4) **Choose appropriate study materials**

Now that you know the subjects to be examined and the relative amount of each subject to be covered, you can choose suitable study materials. For beginning level jobs, or even advanced ones, if you have a pronounced weakness in some aspect of your training, read a modern, standard textbook in that field. Be sure it is up to date and has general coverage. Such books are normally available at your library, and the librarian will be glad to help you locate one. For entry-level positions, questions of appropriate difficulty are chosen – neither highly advanced questions, nor those too simple. Such questions require careful thought but not advanced training.

If the position for which you are applying is technical or advanced, you will read more advanced, specialized material. If you are already familiar with the basic principles of your field, elementary textbooks would waste your time. Concentrate on advanced textbooks and technical periodicals. Think through the concepts and review difficult problems in your field.

These are all general sources. You can get more ideas on your own initiative, following these leads. For example, training manuals and publications of the government agency which employs workers in your field can be useful, particularly for technical and professional positions. A letter or visit to the government department involved may result in more specific study suggestions, and certainly will provide you with a more definite idea of the exact nature of the position you are seeking.

III. KINDS OF TESTS

Tests are used for purposes other than measuring knowledge and ability to perform specified duties. For some positions, it is equally important to test ability to make adjustments to new situations or to profit from training. In others, basic mental abilities not dependent on information are essential. Questions which test these things may not appear as pertinent to the duties of the position as those which test for knowledge and information. Yet they are often highly important parts of a fair examination. For very general questions, it is almost impossible to help you direct your study efforts. What we can do is to point out some of the more common of these general abilities needed in public service positions and describe some typical questions.

1) General information

Broad, general information has been found useful for predicting job success in some kinds of work. This is tested in a variety of ways, from vocabulary lists to questions about current events. Basic background in some field of work, such as sociology or economics, may be sampled in a group of questions. Often these are principles which have become familiar to most persons through exposure rather than through formal training. It is difficult to advise you how to study for these questions; being alert to the world around you is our best suggestion.

2) Verbal ability

An example of an ability needed in many positions is verbal or language ability. Verbal ability is, in brief, the ability to use and understand words. Vocabulary and grammar tests are typical measures of this ability. Reading comprehension or paragraph interpretation questions are common in many kinds of civil service tests. You are given a paragraph of written material and asked to find its central meaning.

3) Numerical ability

Number skills can be tested by the familiar arithmetic problem, by checking paired lists of numbers to see which are alike and which are different, or by interpreting charts and graphs. In the latter test, a graph may be printed in the test booklet which you are asked to use as the basis for answering questions.

4) Observation

A popular test for law-enforcement positions is the observation test. A picture is shown to you for several minutes, then taken away. Questions about the picture test your ability to observe both details and larger elements.

5) Following directions

In many positions in the public service, the employee must be able to carry out written instructions dependably and accurately. You may be given a chart with several columns, each column listing a variety of information. The questions require you to carry out directions involving the information given in the chart.

6) Skills and aptitudes

Performance tests effectively measure some manual skills and aptitudes. When the skill is one in which you are trained, such as typing or shorthand, you can practice. These tests are often very much like those given in business school or high school courses. For many of the other skills and aptitudes, however, no short-time preparation can be made. Skills and abilities natural to you or that you have developed throughout your lifetime are being tested.

Many of the general questions just described provide all the data needed to answer the questions and ask you to use your reasoning ability to find the answers. Your best preparation for these tests, as well as for tests of facts and ideas, is to be at your physical and mental best. You, no doubt, have your own methods of getting into an exam-taking mood and keeping "in shape." The next section lists some ideas on this subject.

IV. KINDS OF QUESTIONS

Only rarely is the "essay" question, which you answer in narrative form, used in civil service tests. Civil service tests are usually of the short-answer type. Full instructions for answering these questions will be given to you at the examination. But in case this is your first experience with short-answer questions and separate answer sheets, here is what you need to know:

1) Multiple-choice Questions

Most popular of the short-answer questions is the "multiple choice" or "best answer" question. It can be used, for example, to test for factual knowledge, ability to solve problems or judgment in meeting situations found at work.

A multiple-choice question is normally one of three types—

- It can begin with an incomplete statement followed by several possible endings. You are to find the one ending which *best* completes the statement, although some of the others may not be entirely wrong.
- It can also be a complete statement in the form of a question which is answered by choosing one of the statements listed.
- It can be in the form of a problem – again you select the best answer.

Here is an example of a multiple-choice question with a discussion which should give you some clues as to the method for choosing the right answer:

When an employee has a complaint about his assignment, the action which will *best* help him overcome his difficulty is to
A. discuss his difficulty with his coworkers
B. take the problem to the head of the organization
C. take the problem to the person who gave him the assignment
D. say nothing to anyone about his complaint

In answering this question, you should study each of the choices to find which is best. Consider choice "A" – Certainly an employee may discuss his complaint with fellow employees, but no change or improvement can result, and the complaint remains unresolved. Choice "B" is a poor choice since the head of the organization probably does not know what assignment you have been given, and taking your problem to him is known as "going over the head" of the supervisor. The supervisor, or person who made the assignment, is the person who can clarify it or correct any injustice. Choice "C" is, therefore, correct. To say nothing, as in choice "D," is unwise. Supervisors have and interest in knowing the problems employees are facing, and the employee is seeking a solution to his problem.

2) True/False Questions

The "true/false" or "right/wrong" form of question is sometimes used. Here a complete statement is given. Your job is to decide whether the statement is right or wrong.

SAMPLE: A roaming cell-phone call to a nearby city costs less than a non-roaming call to a distant city.

This statement is wrong, or false, since roaming calls are more expensive.

This is not a complete list of all possible question forms, although most of the others are variations of these common types. You will always get complete directions for answering questions. Be sure you understand *how* to mark your answers – ask questions until you do.

V. RECORDING YOUR ANSWERS

Computer terminals are used more and more today for many different kinds of exams.

For an examination with very few applicants, you may be told to record your answers in the test booklet itself. Separate answer sheets are much more common. If this separate answer sheet is to be scored by machine – and this is often the case – it is highly important that you mark your answers correctly in order to get credit.

An electronic scoring machine is often used in civil service offices because of the speed with which papers can be scored. Machine-scored answer sheets must be marked with a pencil, which will be given to you. This pencil has a high graphite content which responds to the electronic scoring machine. As a matter of fact, stray dots may register as answers, so do not let your pencil rest on the answer sheet while you are pondering the correct answer. Also, if your pencil lead breaks or is otherwise defective, ask for another.

Since the answer sheet will be dropped in a slot in the scoring machine, be careful not to bend the corners or get the paper crumpled.

The answer sheet normally has five vertical columns of numbers, with 30 numbers to a column. These numbers correspond to the question numbers in your test booklet. After each number, going across the page are four or five pairs of dotted lines. These short dotted lines have small letters or numbers above them. The first two pairs may also have a "T" or "F" above the letters. This indicates that the first two pairs only are to be used if the questions are of the true-false type. If the questions are multiple choice, disregard the "T" and "F" and pay attention only to the small letters or numbers.

Answer your questions in the manner of the sample that follows:

32. The largest city in the United States is
A. Washington, D.C.
B. New York City
C. Chicago
D. Detroit
E. San Francisco

1) Choose the answer you think is best. (New York City is the largest, so "B" is correct.)
2) Find the row of dotted lines numbered the same as the question you are answering. (Find row number 32)
3) Find the pair of dotted lines corresponding to the answer. (Find the pair of lines under the mark "B.")
4) Make a solid black mark between the dotted lines.

VI. BEFORE THE TEST

Common sense will help you find procedures to follow to get ready for an examination. Too many of us, however, overlook these sensible measures. Indeed, nervousness and fatigue have been found to be the most serious reasons why applicants fail to do their best on civil service tests. Here is a list of reminders:

- Begin your preparation early – Don't wait until the last minute to go scurrying around for books and materials or to find out what the position is all about.
- Prepare continuously – An hour a night for a week is better than an all-night cram session. This has been definitely established. What is more, a night a week for a month will return better dividends than crowding your study into a shorter period of time.
- Locate the place of the exam – You have been sent a notice telling you when and where to report for the examination. If the location is in a different town or otherwise unfamiliar to you, it would be well to inquire the best route and learn something about the building.
- Relax the night before the test – Allow your mind to rest. Do not study at all that night. Plan some mild recreation or diversion; then go to bed early and get a good night's sleep.
- Get up early enough to make a leisurely trip to the place for the test – This way unforeseen events, traffic snarls, unfamiliar buildings, etc. will not upset you.
- Dress comfortably – A written test is not a fashion show. You will be known by number and not by name, so wear something comfortable.
- Leave excess paraphernalia at home – Shopping bags and odd bundles will get in your way. You need bring only the items mentioned in the official notice you received; usually everything you need is provided. Do not bring reference books to the exam. They will only confuse those last minutes and be taken away from you when in the test room.
- Arrive somewhat ahead of time – If because of transportation schedules you must get there very early, bring a newspaper or magazine to take your mind off yourself while waiting.
- Locate the examination room – When you have found the proper room, you will be directed to the seat or part of the room where you will sit. Sometimes you are given a sheet of instructions to read while you are waiting. Do not fill out any forms until you are told to do so; just read them and be prepared.
- Relax and prepare to listen to the instructions
- If you have any physical problem that may keep you from doing your best, be sure to tell the test administrator. If you are sick or in poor health, you really cannot do your best on the exam. You can come back and take the test some other time.

VII. AT THE TEST

The day of the test is here and you have the test booklet in your hand. The temptation to get going is very strong. Caution! There is more to success than knowing the right answers. You must know how to identify your papers and understand variations in the type of short-answer question used in this particular examination. Follow these suggestions for maximum results from your efforts:

1) Cooperate with the monitor

The test administrator has a duty to create a situation in which you can be as much at ease as possible. He will give instructions, tell you when to begin, check to see that you are marking your answer sheet correctly, and so on. He is not there to guard you, although he will see that your competitors do not take unfair advantage. He wants to help you do your best.

2) Listen to all instructions

Don't jump the gun! Wait until you understand all directions. In most civil service tests you get more time than you need to answer the questions. So don't be in a hurry. Read each word of instructions until you clearly understand the meaning. Study the examples, listen to all announcements and follow directions. Ask questions if you do not understand what to do.

3) Identify your papers

Civil service exams are usually identified by number only. You will be assigned a number; you must not put your name on your test papers. Be sure to copy your number correctly. Since more than one exam may be given, copy your exact examination title.

4) Plan your time

Unless you are told that a test is a "speed" or "rate of work" test, speed itself is usually not important. Time enough to answer all the questions will be provided, but this does not mean that you have all day. An overall time limit has been set. Divide the total time (in minutes) by the number of questions to determine the approximate time you have for each question.

5) Do not linger over difficult questions

If you come across a difficult question, mark it with a paper clip (useful to have along) and come back to it when you have been through the booklet. One caution if you do this – be sure to skip a number on your answer sheet as well. Check often to be sure that you have not lost your place and that you are marking in the row numbered the same as the question you are answering.

6) Read the questions

Be sure you know what the question asks! Many capable people are unsuccessful because they failed to *read* the questions correctly.

7) Answer all questions

Unless you have been instructed that a penalty will be deducted for incorrect answers, it is better to guess than to omit a question.

8) Speed tests

It is often better NOT to guess on speed tests. It has been found that on timed tests people are tempted to spend the last few seconds before time is called in marking answers at random – without even reading them – in the hope of picking up a few extra points. To discourage this practice, the instructions may warn you that your score will be "corrected" for guessing. That is, a penalty will be applied. The incorrect answers will be deducted from the correct ones, or some other penalty formula will be used.

9) Review your answers

If you finish before time is called, go back to the questions you guessed or omitted to give them further thought. Review other answers if you have time.

10) Return your test materials

If you are ready to leave before others have finished or time is called, take ALL your materials to the monitor and leave quietly. Never take any test material with you. The monitor can discover whose papers are not complete, and taking a test booklet may be grounds for disqualification.

VIII. EXAMINATION TECHNIQUES

1) Read the general instructions carefully. These are usually printed on the first page of the exam booklet. As a rule, these instructions refer to the timing of the examination; the fact that you should not start work until the signal and must stop work at a signal, etc. If there are any *special* instructions, such as a choice of questions to be answered, make sure that you note this instruction carefully.

2) When you are ready to start work on the examination, that is as soon as the signal has been given, read the instructions to each question booklet, underline any key words or phrases, such as *least, best, outline, describe* and the like. In this way you will tend to answer as requested rather than discover on reviewing your paper that you *listed without describing*, that you selected the *worst* choice rather than the *best* choice, etc.

3) If the examination is of the objective or multiple-choice type – that is, each question will also give a series of possible answers: A, B, C or D, and you are called upon to select the best answer and write the letter next to that answer on your answer paper – it is advisable to start answering each question in turn. There may be anywhere from 50 to 100 such questions in the three or four hours allotted and you can see how much time would be taken if you read through all the questions before beginning to answer any. Furthermore, if you come across a question or group of questions which you know would be difficult to answer, it would undoubtedly affect your handling of all the other questions.

4) If the examination is of the essay type and contains but a few questions, it is a moot point as to whether you should read all the questions before starting to answer any one. Of course, if you are given a choice – say five out of seven and the like – then it is essential to read all the questions so you can eliminate the two that are most difficult. If, however, you are asked to answer all the questions, there may be danger in trying to answer the easiest one first because you may find that you will spend too much time on it. The best technique is to answer the first question, then proceed to the second, etc.

5) Time your answers. Before the exam begins, write down the time it started, then add the time allowed for the examination and write down the time it must be completed, then divide the time available somewhat as follows:

- If 3-1/2 hours are allowed, that would be 210 minutes. If you have 80 objective-type questions, that would be an average of 2-1/2 minutes per question. Allow yourself no more than 2 minutes per question, or a total of 160 minutes, which will permit about 50 minutes to review.
- If for the time allotment of 210 minutes there are 7 essay questions to answer, that would average about 30 minutes a question. Give yourself only 25 minutes per question so that you have about 35 minutes to review.

6) The most important instruction is to *read each question* and make sure you know what is wanted. The second most important instruction is to *time yourself properly* so that you answer every question. The third most important instruction is to *answer every question*. Guess if you have to but include something for each question. Remember that you will receive no credit for a blank and will probably receive some credit if you write something in answer to an essay question. If you guess a letter – say "B" for a multiple-choice question – you may have guessed right. If you leave a blank as an answer to a multiple-choice question, the examiners may respect your feelings but it will not add a point to your score. Some exams may penalize you for wrong answers, so in such cases *only*, you may not want to guess unless you have some basis for your answer.

7) Suggestions
    a. Objective-type questions
        1. Examine the question booklet for proper sequence of pages and questions
        2. Read all instructions carefully
        3. Skip any question which seems too difficult; return to it after all other questions have been answered
        4. Apportion your time properly; do not spend too much time on any single question or group of questions
        5. Note and underline key words – *all, most, fewest, least, best, worst, same, opposite,* etc.
        6. Pay particular attention to negatives
        7. Note unusual option, e.g., unduly long, short, complex, different or similar in content to the body of the question
        8. Observe the use of "hedging" words – *probably, may, most likely,* etc.
        9. Make sure that your answer is put next to the same number as the question
        10. Do not second-guess unless you have good reason to believe the second answer is definitely more correct
        11. Cross out original answer if you decide another answer is more accurate; do not erase until you are ready to hand your paper in
        12. Answer all questions; guess unless instructed otherwise
        13. Leave time for review

    b. Essay questions
        1. Read each question carefully
        2. Determine exactly what is wanted. Underline key words or phrases.
        3. Decide on outline or paragraph answer

4. Include many different points and elements unless asked to develop any one or two points or elements
5. Show impartiality by giving pros and cons unless directed to select one side only
6. Make and write down any assumptions you find necessary to answer the questions
7. Watch your English, grammar, punctuation and choice of words
8. Time your answers; don't crowd material

8) Answering the essay question

Most essay questions can be answered by framing the specific response around several key words or ideas. Here are a few such key words or ideas:

M's: manpower, materials, methods, money, management
P's: purpose, program, policy, plan, procedure, practice, problems, pitfalls, personnel, public relations
   a. Six basic steps in handling problems:
      1. Preliminary plan and background development
      2. Collect information, data and facts
      3. Analyze and interpret information, data and facts
      4. Analyze and develop solutions as well as make recommendations
      5. Prepare report and sell recommendations
      6. Install recommendations and follow up effectiveness

   b. Pitfalls to avoid
      1. *Taking things for granted* – A statement of the situation does not necessarily imply that each of the elements is necessarily true; for example, a complaint may be invalid and biased so that all that can be taken for granted is that a complaint has been registered
      2. *Considering only one side of a situation* – Wherever possible, indicate several alternatives and then point out the reasons you selected the best one
      3. *Failing to indicate follow up* – Whenever your answer indicates action on your part, make certain that you will take proper follow-up action to see how successful your recommendations, procedures or actions turn out to be
      4. *Taking too long in answering any single question* – Remember to time your answers properly

IX. AFTER THE TEST

Scoring procedures differ in detail among civil service jurisdictions although the general principles are the same. Whether the papers are hand-scored or graded by machine we have described, they are nearly always graded by number. That is, the person who marks the paper knows only the number – never the name – of the applicant. Not until all the papers have been graded will they be matched with names. If other tests, such as training and experience or oral interview ratings have been given, scores will be combined. Different parts of the examination usually have different weights. For example, the written test might count 60 percent of the final grade, and a rating of training and experience 40 percent. In many jurisdictions, veterans will have a certain number of points added to their grades.

After the final grade has been determined, the names are placed in grade order and an eligible list is established. There are various methods for resolving ties between those who get the same final grade – probably the most common is to place first the name of the person whose application was received first. Job offers are made from the eligible list in the order the names appear on it. You will be notified of your grade and your rank as soon as all these computations have been made. This will be done as rapidly as possible.

People who are found to meet the requirements in the announcement are called "eligibles." Their names are put on a list of eligible candidates. An eligible's chances of getting a job depend on how high he stands on this list and how fast agencies are filling jobs from the list.

When a job is to be filled from a list of eligibles, the agency asks for the names of people on the list of eligibles for that job. When the civil service commission receives this request, it sends to the agency the names of the three people highest on this list. Or, if the job to be filled has specialized requirements, the office sends the agency the names of the top three persons who meet these requirements from the general list.

The appointing officer makes a choice from among the three people whose names were sent to him. If the selected person accepts the appointment, the names of the others are put back on the list to be considered for future openings.

That is the rule in hiring from all kinds of eligible lists, whether they are for typist, carpenter, chemist, or something else. For every vacancy, the appointing officer has his choice of any one of the top three eligibles on the list. This explains why the person whose name is on top of the list sometimes does not get an appointment when some of the persons lower on the list do. If the appointing officer chooses the second or third eligible, the No. 1 eligible does not get a job at once, but stays on the list until he is appointed or the list is terminated.

X. HOW TO PASS THE INTERVIEW TEST

The examination for which you applied requires an oral interview test. You have already taken the written test and you are now being called for the interview test – the final part of the formal examination.

You may think that it is not possible to prepare for an interview test and that there are no procedures to follow during an interview. Our purpose is to point out some things you can do in advance that will help you and some good rules to follow and pitfalls to avoid while you are being interviewed.

What is an interview supposed to test?

The written examination is designed to test the technical knowledge and competence of the candidate; the oral is designed to evaluate intangible qualities, not readily measured otherwise, and to establish a list showing the relative fitness of each candidate – as measured against his competitors – for the position sought. Scoring is not on the basis of "right" and "wrong," but on a sliding scale of values ranging from "not passable" to "outstanding." As a matter of fact, it is possible to achieve a relatively low score without a single "incorrect" answer because of evident weakness in the qualities being measured.

Occasionally, an examination may consist entirely of an oral test – either an individual or a group oral. In such cases, information is sought concerning the technical knowledges and abilities of the candidate, since there has been no written examination for this purpose. More commonly, however, an oral test is used to supplement a written examination.

Who conducts interviews?

The composition of oral boards varies among different jurisdictions. In nearly all, a representative of the personnel department serves as chairman. One of the members of the board may be a representative of the department in which the candidate would work. In some cases, "outside experts" are used, and, frequently, a businessman or some other representative of the general public is asked to serve. Labor and management or other special groups may be represented. The aim is to secure the services of experts in the appropriate field.

However the board is composed, it is a good idea (and not at all improper or unethical) to ascertain in advance of the interview who the members are and what groups they represent. When you are introduced to them, you will have some idea of their backgrounds and interests, and at least you will not stutter and stammer over their names.

What should be done before the interview?

While knowledge about the board members is useful and takes some of the surprise element out of the interview, there is other preparation which is more substantive. It *is* possible to prepare for an oral interview – in several ways:

1) Keep a copy of your application and review it carefully before the interview

This may be the only document before the oral board, and the starting point of the interview. Know what education and experience you have listed there, and the sequence and dates of all of it. Sometimes the board will ask you to review the highlights of your experience for them; you should not have to hem and haw doing it.

2) Study the class specification and the examination announcement

Usually, the oral board has one or both of these to guide them. The qualities, characteristics or knowledges required by the position sought are stated in these documents. They offer valuable clues as to the nature of the oral interview. For example, if the job involves supervisory responsibilities, the announcement will usually indicate that knowledge of modern supervisory methods and the qualifications of the candidate as a supervisor will be tested. If so, you can expect such questions, frequently in the form of a hypothetical situation which you are expected to solve. NEVER go into an oral without knowledge of the duties and responsibilities of the job you seek.

3) Think through each qualification required

Try to visualize the kind of questions you would ask if you were a board member. How well could you answer them? Try especially to appraise your own knowledge and background in each area, *measured against the job sought*, and identify any areas in which you are weak. Be critical and realistic – do not flatter yourself.

4) Do some general reading in areas in which you feel you may be weak

For example, if the job involves supervision and your past experience has NOT, some general reading in supervisory methods and practices, particularly in the field of human relations, might be useful. Do NOT study agency procedures or detailed manuals. The oral board will be testing your understanding and capacity, not your memory.

5) Get a good night's sleep and watch your general health and mental attitude

You will want a clear head at the interview. Take care of a cold or any other minor ailment, and of course, no hangovers.

What should be done on the day of the interview?

Now comes the day of the interview itself. Give yourself plenty of time to get there. Plan to arrive somewhat ahead of the scheduled time, particularly if your appointment is in the fore part of the day. If a previous candidate fails to appear, the board might be ready for you a bit early. By early afternoon an oral board is almost invariably behind schedule if there are many candidates, and you may have to wait. Take along a book or magazine to read, or your application to review, but leave any extraneous material in the waiting room when you go in for your interview. In any event, relax and compose yourself.

The matter of dress is important. The board is forming impressions about you – from your experience, your manners, your attitude, and your appearance. Give your personal appearance careful attention. Dress your best, but not your flashiest. Choose conservative, appropriate clothing, and be sure it is immaculate. This is a business interview, and your appearance should indicate that you regard it as such. Besides, being well groomed and properly dressed will help boost your confidence.

Sooner or later, someone will call your name and escort you into the interview room. *This is it.* From here on you are on your own. It is too late for any more preparation. But remember, you asked for this opportunity to prove your fitness, and you are here because your request was granted.

What happens when you go in?

The usual sequence of events will be as follows: The clerk (who is often the board stenographer) will introduce you to the chairman of the oral board, who will introduce you to the other members of the board. Acknowledge the introductions before you sit down. Do not be surprised if you find a microphone facing you or a stenotypist sitting by. Oral interviews are usually recorded in the event of an appeal or other review.

Usually the chairman of the board will open the interview by reviewing the highlights of your education and work experience from your application – primarily for the benefit of the other members of the board, as well as to get the material into the record. Do not interrupt or comment unless there is an error or significant misinterpretation; if that is the case, do not hesitate. But do not quibble about insignificant matters. Also, he will usually ask you some question about your education, experience or your present job – partly to get you to start talking and to establish the interviewing "rapport." He may start the actual questioning, or turn it over to one of the other members. Frequently, each member undertakes the questioning on a particular area, one in which he is perhaps most competent, so you can expect each member to participate in the examination. Because time is limited, you may also expect some rather abrupt switches in the direction the questioning takes, so do not be upset by it. Normally, a board member will not pursue a single line of questioning unless he discovers a particular strength or weakness.

After each member has participated, the chairman will usually ask whether any member has any further questions, then will ask you if you have anything you wish to add. Unless you are expecting this question, it may floor you. Worse, it may start you off on an extended, extemporaneous speech. The board is not usually seeking more information. The question is principally to offer you a last opportunity to present further qualifications or to indicate that you have nothing to add. So, if you feel that a significant qualification or characteristic has been overlooked, it is proper to point it out in a sentence or so. Do not compliment the board on the thoroughness of their examination – they have been sketchy, and you know it. If you wish, merely say, "No thank you, I have nothing further to add." This is a point where you can "talk yourself out" of a good impression or fail to present an important bit of information. Remember, *you close the interview yourself.*

The chairman will then say, "That is all, Mr. _____, thank you." Do not be startled; the interview is over, and quicker than you think. Thank him, gather your belongings and take your leave. Save your sigh of relief for the other side of the door.

How to put your best foot forward

Throughout this entire process, you may feel that the board individually and collectively is trying to pierce your defenses, seek out your hidden weaknesses and embarrass and confuse you. Actually, this is not true. They are obliged to make an appraisal of your qualifications for the job you are seeking, and they want to see you in your best light. Remember, they must interview all candidates and a non-cooperative candidate may become a failure in spite of their best efforts to bring out his qualifications. Here are 15 suggestions that will help you:

1) Be natural – Keep your attitude confident, not cocky

If you are not confident that you can do the job, do not expect the board to be. Do not apologize for your weaknesses, try to bring out your strong points. The board is interested in a positive, not negative, presentation. Cockiness will antagonize any board member and make him wonder if you are covering up a weakness by a false show of strength.

2) Get comfortable, but don't lounge or sprawl

Sit erectly but not stiffly. A careless posture may lead the board to conclude that you are careless in other things, or at least that you are not impressed by the importance of the occasion. Either conclusion is natural, even if incorrect. Do not fuss with your clothing, a pencil or an ashtray. Your hands may occasionally be useful to emphasize a point; do not let them become a point of distraction.

3) Do not wisecrack or make small talk

This is a serious situation, and your attitude should show that you consider it as such. Further, the time of the board is limited – they do not want to waste it, and neither should you.

4) Do not exaggerate your experience or abilities

In the first place, from information in the application or other interviews and sources, the board may know more about you than you think. Secondly, you probably will not get away with it. An experienced board is rather adept at spotting such a situation, so do not take the chance.

5) If you know a board member, do not make a point of it, yet do not hide it

Certainly you are not fooling him, and probably not the other members of the board. Do not try to take advantage of your acquaintanceship – it will probably do you little good.

6) Do not dominate the interview

Let the board do that. They will give you the clues – do not assume that you have to do all the talking. Realize that the board has a number of questions to ask you, and do not try to take up all the interview time by showing off your extensive knowledge of the answer to the first one.

7) Be attentive

You only have 20 minutes or so, and you should keep your attention at its sharpest throughout. When a member is addressing a problem or question to you, give him your undivided attention. Address your reply principally to him, but do not exclude the other board members.

8) Do not interrupt

A board member may be stating a problem for you to analyze. He will ask you a question when the time comes. Let him state the problem, and wait for the question.

9) Make sure you understand the question

Do not try to answer until you are sure what the question is. If it is not clear, restate it in your own words or ask the board member to clarify it for you. However, do not haggle about minor elements.

10) Reply promptly but not hastily

A common entry on oral board rating sheets is "candidate responded readily," or "candidate hesitated in replies." Respond as promptly and quickly as you can, but do not jump to a hasty, ill-considered answer.

11) Do not be peremptory in your answers

A brief answer is proper – but do not fire your answer back. That is a losing game from your point of view. The board member can probably ask questions much faster than you can answer them.

12) Do not try to create the answer you think the board member wants

He is interested in what kind of mind you have and how it works – not in playing games. Furthermore, he can usually spot this practice and will actually grade you down on it.

13) Do not switch sides in your reply merely to agree with a board member

Frequently, a member will take a contrary position merely to draw you out and to see if you are willing and able to defend your point of view. Do not start a debate, yet do not surrender a good position. If a position is worth taking, it is worth defending.

14) Do not be afraid to admit an error in judgment if you are shown to be wrong

The board knows that you are forced to reply without any opportunity for careful consideration. Your answer may be demonstrably wrong. If so, admit it and get on with the interview.

15) Do not dwell at length on your present job

The opening question may relate to your present assignment. Answer the question but do not go into an extended discussion. You are being examined for a *new* job, not your present one. As a matter of fact, try to phrase ALL your answers in terms of the job for which you are being examined.

Basis of Rating

Probably you will forget most of these "do's" and "don'ts" when you walk into the oral interview room. Even remembering them all will not ensure you a passing grade. Perhaps you did not have the qualifications in the first place. But remembering them will help you to put your best foot forward, without treading on the toes of the board members.

Rumor and popular opinion to the contrary notwithstanding, an oral board wants you to make the best appearance possible. They know you are under pressure – but they also want to see how you respond to it as a guide to what your reaction would be under the pressures of the job you seek. They will be influenced by the degree of poise you display, the personal traits you show and the manner in which you respond.

ABOUT THIS BOOK

This book contains tests divided into Examination Sections. Go through each test, answering every question in the margin. At the end of each test look at the answer key and check your answers. On the ones you got wrong, look at the right answer choice and learn. Do not fill in the answers first. Do not memorize the questions and answers, but understand the answer and principles involved. On your test, the questions will likely be different from the samples. Questions are changed and new ones added. If you understand these past questions you should have success with any changes that arise. Tests may consist of several types of questions. We have additional books on each subject should more study be advisable or necessary for you. Finally, the more you study, the better prepared you will be. This book is intended to be the last thing you study before you walk into the examination room. Prior study of relevant texts is also recommended. NLC publishes some of these in our Fundamental Series. Knowledge and good sense are important factors in passing your exam. Good luck also helps. So now study this Passbook, absorb the material contained within and take that knowledge into the examination. Then do your best to pass that exam.

———

EXAMINATION SECTION

EXAMINATION SECTION
TEST 1

DIRECTIONS: Each question or incomplete statement is followed by several suggested answers or completions. Select the one that BEST answers the question or completes the statement. *PRINT THE LETTER OF THE CORRECT ANSWER IN THE SPACE AT THE RIGHT.*

1. A shrink fitted collar is to be removed from a shaft. One good way to do this would be to drive out the shaft after _____ collar.

    A. *chilling* only the
    B. *chilling* both the shaft and
    C. *heating* only the
    D. *heating* both the shaft and

1.____

2. It is CORRECT to say that

    A. a standard brick weighs about 8 lbs.
    B. the dimensions of a common brick are 8" x 3 3/4" x 2 1/4"
    C. vertical joints in a brick wall are called bed joints
    D. in laying bricks the head joints should be slushed with mortar

2.____

3. A snail pump impeller is checked for static balance by

    A. running the pump at high speed and listening for rubs
    B. mounting it on parallel and level knife edges and noting if it turns
    C. weighing it and comparing the weight against the original weight
    D. putting it on a lathe to see if it runs true

3.____

4. The sum of the following dimensions: 3' x 2 1/4", 8 7/8", 2'6 3/8", 2'9 3/4", and 1'0" is

    A. 16'7 1/4"   B. 10'7 1/4"   C. 10'3 1/4"   D. 9'3 1/4"

4.____

5. A requisition for nails was worded as follows: *100 lbs., 10d, 3 inch, common wive nails, galvanized.*
The UNNECESSARY information in this requisition is

    A. 100 lbs.   B. common   C. galvanized   D. 3 inch

5.____

6. Electric arc welding is COMMONLY done by the use of _____ voltage and _____ amperage.

    A. *low; high*   B. *high; high*
    C. *high; low*   D. *low; low*

6.____

7. A GOOD principle for you to follow after teaching a maintenance procedure to a new helper is to

    A. tell him that you expect him to make many mistakes at first
    B. observe his work procedure and point out any errors he may make
    C. have him write out the procedure from memory
    D. assume he knows the procedure if he asks no questions

7.____

8. Multiple threads are used on the stems of some large valves to   8.____

    A. reduce the effort required to open the valve
    B. prevent binding of the valve stem
    C. secure faster opening and closing of the valve
    D. decrease the length of stem travel

9. After the base plate of a new machine has been fitted over the foundation bolts, it should   9.____
    be leveled by

    A. inserting steel shims under the plate
    B. chipping the high spots off the floor
    C. using thin cement grout under the plate
    D. grinding down the high spots on the base plate

10. In nixing concrete by hand, the materials are first thoroughly mixed dry and then mixed   10.____
    with water. This is a good procedure because it

    A. caves cement
    B. reduces the amount of water required
    C. avoids settling of the aggregate
    D. properly coats the aggregate with the cement

11. A revolution counter applied to the end of a rotating shaft reads 100 when a stopwatch is   11.____
    started and 850 after 90 seconds.
    The shaft is rotating at a speed of _____ rpm.

    A. 500   B. 633   C. 750   D. 950

12. If a kink develops in a wire rope, it would be BEST to   12.____

    A. hammer out the kink with a lead hammer
    B. straighten out the kink by putting it in a vise and applying sufficient pressure
    C. discard the portion of the rope containing the kink
    D. keep the rope in use and allow the kink to work itself out

13. Steel pipe posts have been placed into prepared holes in concrete.   13.____
    To properly secure the posts, they should be caulked inplace with

    A. molten lead   B. cement mortar
    C. oakum   D. hot pitch

14. The PRINCIPAL reason for grounding of electrical equipment is to   14.____

    A. save power   B. guard against shock
    C. prevent open circuits   D. prevent short circuits

15. A spirit level has been dropped and a deep indentation made in the wood.   15.____
    The BEST thing to do is to

    A. ignore the incident if the bubbles were not broken
    B. sand down the surface to remove the indentation
    C. get a new level
    D. test the level

16. A strike plate is MOST closely associated with a 16._____

    A. lock
    B. sash weight
    C. hinge
    D. door check

17. You receive a special assignment from your superior calling for the use of a type of wood 17._____
which in your opinion is not suitable for the job.
You should

    A. substitute the wood you believe to be most suitable
    B. carry out the order as received
    C. immediately call this to his attention
    D. consult another maintainer on what to do

18. A motor driven centrifugal pump takes water from a city main and delivers it to the noz- 18._____
zles of a train washing machine. With little change in motor speed or suction pressure,
the discharge pressure rises and the flow of cleaning water falls to a trickle.
The PROBABLE cause is a

    A. failure of the impeller shaft
    B. leak in the piping between the pressure gage point of attachment and the nozzles
    C. blockage of the impeller
    D. blockage between the pressure gage point of attachment and the nozzles

19. A standard hoisting rope size is designated as 6 x 19. This indicates that the rope has 19._____

    A. 6 strands, each made of 19 wires
    B. 19 strands, each made of 6 wires
    C. 6 strands of No. 19 gage wire
    D. 19 strands of No. 6 gage wire

20. The two planes which make up the MOST useful combination 20._____
for general carpentry work are the _____ plane and the _____ plane.

    A. jack; jointer
    B. jack; block
    C. smooth; block
    D. fore; jointer

21. If you were drilling a structural plate and the drill cuttings were in the form of long contin- 21._____
uous shavings, you could rightly conclude that the

    A. drill point was too sharp
    B. material being drilled was wrought iron
    C. bearing pressure on the drill was insufficient
    D. drilling was being done correctly

22. Studs and joists for light building construction are USUALLY spaced on _____ inch cen- 22._____
ters.

    A. 12
    B. 14
    C. 16
    D. 18

23. If power driven rivets are loose, the MOST likely reason would be that the rivets were 23._____

    A. too long
    B. too short
    C. driven with high air pressure
    D. overheated

24. If a drawing for a pipe installation is made to a scale of 1 1/2" to the foot, the drawing is said to be one _____ size.

    A. half   B. quarter   C. eighth   D. sixteenth

24.____

25. A gear train consists of a driver with 120 teeth, an idler with 60 teeth, and a driven gear with 200 teeth. If the driver rotates at 1500 rpm, the driven gear rotates at _____ rpm.

    A. 225   B. 900   C. 2500   D. 10,000

25.____

26. A certain pipe fitting is marked *200 WOG*. This fitting could NOT properly be used in a pipe line for _____ pounds gage maximum.

    A. steam at 200   B. water at 150
    C. air at 200   D. oil at 150

26.____

27. A file having two *safe* edges is COMMONLY known as a _____ file.

    A. flat   B. mill   C. hand   D. pillar

27.____

28. By trial, it is found that by using 2 cubic feet of sand, a 5 cubic foot batch of concrete is produced.
Using the same proportions, the amount of sand, in cubic feet, required to produce 2 cubic yards of concrete is MOST NEARLY

    A. 7   B. 22   C. 27   D. 45

28.____

29. Tooling of the face joints of a brick wall under construction should be done

    A. after the mortar has acquired its initial set
    B. after the entire wall is laid
    C. after the mortar has acquired its final set
    D. as each brick is laid

29.____

30. A gland bushing is associated in practice with a(n)

    A. gas engine   B. electric motor
    C. centrifugal pump   D. lathe

30.____

31. A house drain is successively offset by means of a 1/8 bend, a 1/16 bend, and a 1/32 bend.
The total angular offset of this line is MOST NEARLY

    A. 34°   B. 39°   C. 68°   D. 79°

31.____

32. The flushing mechanism in a low tank water closet is so arranged that a fill tube supplies water from the ball cock to the overflow standpipe for a short interval immediately after the closet is flushed.
The MAIN reason for this is to

    A. finish cleaning the water passages of the closet
    B. properly seal the ball in its seat
    C. renew the seal in the closet trap
    D. scour the flush tube from the tank to the closet

32.____

33. A job calls for the setting of wrought iron pipe sleeves in concrete floor construction for the passage of water risers.
In order to provide for the passage of a 2" riser, the MINIMUM diameter of the sleeve is

    A. 2 1/2"   B. 3"   C. 4"   D. 5"

33._____

34. When applied to lumber, the designation *S4S* means

    A. all sides are rough
    B. all four sides are of the same size
    C. fourth grade lumber
    D. all sides are dressed

34._____

35. To guard against accidents in connection with wood scaffolding,

    A. inspect the nailing before the scaffold is loaded
    B. never put a heavy load on a scaffold
    C. use only heavy timber for scaffold construction
    D. do not build high scaffolds

35._____

36. A reducing tee has one run opening of 2 inches, the second run opening of 14 inches, and the branch opening of 1 inch.
This tee would be specified as

    A. 1 x 1 1/2 x 2   B. 1 x 2 x 1 1/2
    C. 2 x 1 1/2 x 1   D. 2 x 1 x 1 1/2

36._____

37. A length of pipe is to be fitted with a 90° elbow at each end. The center to center distance between elbows is to be 4'6". The center to end dimension of each elbow is 2" and the thread engagement is 1/2".
The length to which the pipe should be cut is

    A. 4'1"   B. 4'2"   C. 4'3"   D. 4'4 1/2"

37._____

38. Sheet metal seams are sometimes grooved. The MAIN function of the grooving is to

    A. facilitate making a soldered joint
    B. prevent unlocking
    C. improve the appearance of the joint
    D. save sheet metal

38._____

39. When fitting new piston rings in a compressor, the piston ring gap is BEST measured by means of a(n)

    A. feeler gage   B. inside caliper
    C. 6" rule   D. depth gage

39._____

40. The ampere-hour rating of a battery depends MAINLY on the

    A. number of cells connected in series
    B. casing composition
    C. quantity of electrolyte
    D. number and area of the battery plates

40._____

KEY (CORRECT ANSWERS)

1.	C	11.	A	21.	D	31.	D
2.	B	12.	C	22.	C	32.	C
3.	B	13.	A	23.	B	33.	B
4.	C	14.	B	24.	C	34.	D
5.	D	15.	D	25.	B	35.	A
6.	A	16.	A	26.	A	36.	C
7.	B	17.	C	27.	D	37.	C
8.	C	18.	D	28.	B	38.	B
9.	A	19.	A	29.	A	39.	A
10.	D	20.	B	30.	C	40.	D

TEST 2

DIRECTIONS: Each question or incomplete statement is followed by several suggested answers or completions. Select the one that BEST answers the question or completes the statement. *PRINT THE LETTER OF THE CORRECT ANSWER IN THE SPACE AT THE RIGHT.*

1. In making a high wooden scaffold, proper splices in 2 x 4 lumber which is to be used vertically would be made by   1.____

   A. lapping each joint with a cleat below
   B. butting the ends and boxing in the joints with 1" boards
   C. butting the ends and nailing a 2 x 4 over the splice
   D. making half-lap joints

2. With respect to soldering, it is LEAST important that   2.____

   A. the soldering copper be clean and well-tinned
   B. a good flux suitable for the metal being soldered be used
   C. the joint to be soldered be well-cleaned
   D. a lot of solder be used

3. When two sheet metal plates are riveted together, a specified minimum distance must be provided from the edge of each plate to the nearest line of rivets in order to prevent   3.____

   A. the rivet heads from working loose
   B. the rivets from being sheared
   C. tearing of the material between the rivets and the edges of the plates
   D. excessive stress on the rivets

4. A hoisting cable is wound on a 14" drum which is rotating at 5 rpm.
   The load being raised by this cable will move at an APPROXIMATE linear speed, in feet per minute, of   4.____

   A. 13.5   B. 18.3   C. 70   D. 220

5. Spreaders are used in connection with forms for concrete to   5.____

   A. hold the walls of a form the correct distance apart
   B. anchor a form to the ground
   C. make a form watertight
   D. make the cement spread evenly through the form

6. By curing of concrete is meant   6.____

   A. finishing the surface of the concrete
   B. softening stiff concrete by adding water
   C. keeping the concrete wet while setting
   D. the salvaging of frozen concrete

7. If steel weighs 480 lbs. per cubic foot, the weight of an 18" x 18" x 2" steel base plate is _____ lbs.   7.____

   A. 180   B. 216   C. 427   D. 648

8. Standard wrought iron pipe and extra strong wrought iron pipe of the same nominal size differ in

    A. outside diameter   B. inside diameter
    C. chemical composition   D. threading

8.___

9. Plunbing system stacks are vented to the atmosphere. These stacks will NOT

    A. relieve the back pressure on traps from the sewer side
    B. prevent the siphoning of traps
    C. ventilate the drainage system
    D. prevent the sewer from backing up into the fixtures

9.___

10. The MOST likely cause of accidents involving minor injuries is

    A. careless work practices
    B. lack of safety devices
    C. inferior equipment and material
    D. insufficient safety posters

10.___

11. In the maintenance of shop equipment, lubrication should be done

    A. periodically
    B. only if necessary
    C. whenever time permits
    D. only during the overhaul period

11.___

12. The total number of cubic yards of earth to be removed to nake a trench 3'9" wide, 25'0" long, and 4'3" deep is MOST NEARLY

    A. 53.1   B. 35.4   C. 26.6   D. 11.8

12.___

13. A large number of 2 x 4 studs, some 10'5" long and some 6'5 1/2" long, are required for a job.
To minimize waste, it would be preferable to order lengths of _____ ft.

    A. 16   B. 17   C. 18   D. 19

13.___

14. A 6" pipe is connected to a 4" pipe through a reducer. If 100 cubic feet of water is flowing through the 6" pipe per minute, the flow, in cubic feet per minute, through the 4" pipe is

    A. 225   B. 100   C. 66.6   D. 44.4

14.___

15. The type of seam generally used in the construction of sheet metal cylinders of small diameters is the _____ seam.

    A. double edged   B. folded
    C. double hemmed   D. simple lap

15.___

16. Two branch ventilating ducts, one 12 inches square and the other 18 inches square, are to connect to a square main duct.
In order to maintain the same cross-sectional area, the dimension of the main duct should be _____ inches square.

    A. 14   B. 20   C. 24   D. 28

16.___

17. In reference to preparing mortar, it is CORRECT to say that the lime used   17.____

    A. may burn the skin
    B. hastens setting
    C. prevents absorption of water by the brick
    D. decreases the amount of water needed

18. The intercooler of a two-stage air compressor is connected to the, compressor unit   18.____

    A. before the air intake pipe to the first stage
    B. between the second stage and the receiver
    C. between the two stages
    D. after the receiver .

19. In oxyacetylene welding, the hose that is connected to the oxygen cylinder is USUALLY colored   19.____

    A. yellow   B. white   C. purple   D. green

20. When bonding new concrete to old concrete, the surface of the old concrete should be   20.____

    A. left untouched   B. dry
    C. carefully smoothed   D. chipped and roughened

21. A sack of Portland cement is considered to have a volume, in cubic feet, of   21.____

    A. 1/2   B. 3/4   C. 1   D. 14

22. The purpose of a vacuum breaker used with an automatic flush valve is to   22.____

    A. limit the flow of water to the fixture
    B. prevent pollution of the water supply
    C. equalize the water pressure
    D. control the water pressure to the fixture

23. Wiping solder for lead pipe USUALLY has a melting range of _____°F.   23.____

    A. 150 to 250   B. 251 to 350
    C. 360 to 470   D. 475 to 600

24. A space heater is to be suspended from a structural beam. The heater should be suspended by a hanger   24.____

    A. passing through a hole in the web of the beam
    B. passing through a hole in the flange of the beam
    C. welded to the beam
    D. clamped to the beam

25. With respect to babbitted sleeve bearings, oil grooves are   25.____

    A. cut only on the top half
    B. cut only on the bottom half
    C. cut on both halves
    D. never necessary

26. When an employee finds it necessary to work near a live third rail, it is BEST to cover the   26.____
    third rail with a

    A. rubber mat   B. canvas cloth
    C. board   D. sheet of heavy paper

27. A 10-inch foundation wall is 11 feet long and 15 feet high. If the compressive strength of   27.____
    the wall is 300 pounds per square inch, the MAXIMUM permissible load on this wall is
    _____ lbs.

    A. 540,000   B. 495,000   C. 396,000   D. 33,000

28. It is INCORRECT to state that   28.____

    A. neat cement contains cement and water
    B. salt is used to hasten the setting of concrete
    C. the strength of concrete is affected by the water ratio
    D. a sidewalk should slope toward the street

29. When sharpening a hand saw, the FIRST operation is to file the teeth so that they are of   29.____
    the same height. This is known as

    A. shaping   B. setting   C. leveling   D. jointing

30. The swing of a lathe is the   30.____

    A. diameter of the largest piece that can be turned
    B. distance between centers of the head and tail spindles
    C. size of the face plate
    D. radius of the chuck

31. Assume that the lead screw, stud gear, and spindle of a lathe revolve at the same speed.   31.____
    It is required to cut 10 threads per inch when the lead screw has 6 threads per inch.
    If the stud gear has 48 teeth, the lead screw gear must have _____teeth.

    A. 48   B. 60   C. 64   D. 80

32. The safety device used on a crane to prevent overtravel is called a(n)   32.____

    A. unloader   B. governor
    C. limit switch   D. overload relay

33. It is INCORRECT to say that   33.____

    A. there is a difference between fittings for threaded drainage pipe and fittings for ordi-
        nary threaded pipe
    B. a gasoline torch must be fully filled with gasoline
    C. *Red Brass* pipe contains about 85% copper
    D. loose parts in a faucet may cause noisy operation

34. A requisition for lag screws does NOT require stating the   34.____

    A. diameter   B. quantity
    C. threads per inch   D. length

35. In an accident report, the information which may be MOST useful in decreasing the recurrence of similar type accidents is the

    A. extent of injuries sustained
    B. time the accident happened
    C. number of people involved
    D. cause of the accident

35.____

36. Carbon tetrachloride is NOT recommended for cleaning purposes because of

    A. the poisonous nature of its fumes
    B. its limited cleaning value
    C. the damaging effects it has on equipment
    D. the difficulty of application

36.____

37. The part of the thread directly measured with a thread micrometer is the

    A. thread height   B. major diameter
    C. thread lead   D. pitch diameter

37.____

38. The side support for steps or stairs is called a

    A. ledger board   B. runner
    C. stringer   D. riser

38.____

39. A sheet metal plate has been cut in the form of a right triangle with sides of 5, 12, and 13 inches.
The area of this plate, in square inches, is

    A. 30   B. 32 1/2   C. 60   D. 78

39.____

40. The BEST first aid for a man who has no external injury but is apparently suffering from internal injury due to an accident is to

    A. take him at once to a doctor's office
    B. make him comfortable and immediately summon a doctor or ambulance
    C. administer a stimulant
    D. start artificial respiration

40.____

KEY (CORRECT ANSWERS)

1.	B	11.	A	21.	C	31.	D
2.	D	12.	D	22.	B	32.	C
3.	C	13.	C	23.	C	33.	B
4.	B	14.	B	24.	D	34.	C
5.	A	15.	D	25.	A	35.	D
6.	C	16.	B	26.	A	36.	A
7.	A	17.	A	27.	C	37.	D
8.	B	18.	C	28.	B	38.	C
9.	D	19.	D	29.	D	39.	A
10.	A	20.	D	30.	A	40.	B

─────

EXAMINATION SECTION
TEST 1

DIRECTIONS: Each question or incomplete statement is followed by several suggested answers or completions. Select the one that BEST answers the question or completes the statement. *PRINT THE LETTER OF THE CORRECT ANSWER IN THE SPACE AT THE RIGHT.*

1. Of the following, the one that is a grease fitting is a _____ fitting.   1.____

   A. Morse   B. Brown and Sharpe
   C. Zerk   D. Caliper

2. In an automobile equipped with an ammeter, the ammeter is used to   2.____

   A. indicate current flow
   B. regulate current flow
   C. act as a circuit breaker
   D. measure engine r.p.m.

3. The ignition points in the distributor of a gasoline engine are opened by means of a   3.____

   A. spring   B. vacuum
   C. cam with lobes   D. gear

4. MOST automobile engines that use gasoline as fuel operate as _____ cycle engines.   4.____

   A. single   B. single stroke, single
   C. two-stroke, two-   D. four-stroke, two-

5. When making a hole in a concrete floor for a machine hold-down bolt, the BEST tool to use is a   5.____

   A. star drill   B. drift punch
   C. cold chisel   D. counterboring tool

6. When cutting a hole through a 1/2-inch thick wooden partition, the BEST type of saw to use from among the following choices is a _____ saw.   6.____

   A. coping   B. back   C. rip   D. saber

7. An anodized finish is USUALLY associated with   7.____

   A. aluminum   B. steel
   C. cast iron   D. brass

8. Certain devices are used to transmit power from one shaft to another. A device that does so WITHOUT the use of friction is a   8.____

   A. square jaw clutch   B. simple disk clutch
   C. compression coupling   D. thermocouple

9. If it is necessary to check the true temperature setting of a thermostat for a shop unit heater, it would be BEST to use   9.____

   A. a mercury thermometer near the heater
   B. a mercury thermometer near the thermostat

C. another similar thermostat near the thermostat to be tested
D. a standard thermostat

10. To remove a shrink-fitted collar from a shaft, it would be EASIEST to drive out the shaft after   10.____

    A. *chilling* the collar and heating the shaft
    B. *chilling* only the collar
    C. *heating* only the collar
    D. *heating* both the collar and the shaft

11. When drilling a hole in a broken machine stud in order to remove the stud with an extrac-   11.____
tor, it is BEST to drill the hole

    A. off-center
    B. in the center
    C. with the smallest diameter drill possible
    D. with a taper

12. When fitting two steel parts together, steel dowel pins are GENERALLY used to   12.____

    A. keep the parts securely fastened together
    B. provide a wide tolerance fit
    C. provide an adjustable clearance space between the two parts
    D. secure exact placement of these parts with respect to each other

13. When storing files, it is important that they do not touch each other.   13.____
The PRIMARY reason for this is to prevent

    A. damage to the handles
    B. dirt from collecting in the teeth
    C. damage to the teeth
    D. rusting

14. The frequency of lubrication of bearings and other moving parts of machinery depends   14.____
PRIMARILY on

    A. the amount of their use   B. their size
    C. the direction of motion   D. the operator's judgment

15. To determine whether the surface of a work bench is horizontal, the BEST tool to use is a   15.____

    A. surface gage   B. plumb bob
    C. feeler gage   D. spirit level

16. The swing on a lathe refers to the   16.____

    A. distance between centers of the head and tail spindles
    B. size of the face plate
    C. speed range of the gears in r.p.m.
    D. diameter of the largest workpiece that can be turned

17. When installing new piston rings in an air compressor, the piston ring gap is BEST measured by using a(n)   17.____

    A. outside caliper   B. feeler gage
    C. depth gage   D. inside caliper

18. When cutting external threads on a pipe, the tool that ACTUALLY cuts the thread is called a   18.____

    A. tap   B. die   C. reamer   D. hone

19. A dynamometer would be MOST useful in   19.____

    A. measuring angles on a steel plate
    B. determining the operating efficiency of an engine
    C. pumping hot fluids out of a tank
    D. heating large shop areas

20. A screw-thread micrometer is used PRIMARILY to measure   20.____

    A. pitch diameter   B. thread height
    C. major diameter   D. thread lead

21. A compound-pressure gage found on certain types of equipment is used to indicate   21.____

    A. the sum of two pressures
    B. the difference between two pressures
    C. either vacuum or pressure
    D. two different pressures simultaneously

22. Of the following, the machine screw having the SMALLEST diameter is   22.____

    A. 6-32 x 11/2"   B. 8-32 x 3/4"
    C. 10-24 x 1"   D. 12-24 x1/2"

23. A good quality precision compression spring would MOST probably have   23.____

    A. a small diameter and small wire size
    B. its ends ground flat
    C. a large diameter and large wire size
    D. a high spring rate

24. From among the following materials, the MOST fireproof one for use in maintenance work is   24.____

    A. canvas   B. nylon   C. cotton   D. asbestos

25. The metal which has the GREATEST tendency to crack when dropped onto a hard surface is   25.____

    A. rolled steel   B. forged steel
    C. wrought iron   D. cast iron

26. When using a portable electric drill having a 3-conductor cord, it is IMPORTANT from a safety point of view that   26.____

    A. the drill is run at fairly slow speeds
    B. high-speed drill bits should be used

C. the power outlet has a ground connection
D. the drill is run on 3-phase current

27. The MOST efficient way of laying out a 25-foot long, straight line on a concrete floor is to   27.____

    A. use a carpenter's pencil and a steel tape
    B. lay out a cord and mark the line with a crayon
    C. use chalk and a 6-foot ruler
    D. snap it on with a chalked mason's line

28. The MAIN advantage of using pipes instead of timber for temporary scaffolding is that   28.____
pipe scaffolding

    A. requires no painting
    B. is easier to assemble and disassemble
    C. requires no bracing
    D. looks better

29. In order to avoid damage to an air compressor, the air coming into it is USUALLY   29.____

    A. cooled   B. metered   C. filtered   D. heated

30. If a gear having 24 teeth is revolving at 150 r.p.m., then the speed of an 8-tooth pinion   30.____
driving the gear is _____ r.p.m.

    A. 50   B. 300   C. 450   D. 1200

31. To preserve wood from rotting, it is BEST to use   31.____

    A. aluminum paint   B. red lead
    C. rosin   D. creosote

32. On a two-stage air compressor, the intercooler is connected to the compressor unit   32.____

    A. *between* the two stages
    B. *after* the second stage
    C. *before* the first stage
    D. *between* the receiver and the outlet

33. Teflon is COMMONLY used as a(n)   33.____

    A. protective coating on ceramic plumbing fixtures
    B. sealer on threaded pipe joints
    C. additive to engine lubricating oil
    D. penetrating oil for rusting parts

34. A marline spike is GENERALLY used to   34.____

    A. splice manila rope
    B. fasten a heavy metal part to a wood panel wall
    C. shift large crates
    D. anchor wooden items to a concrete wall

35. A screw having double threads is one that   35._____

    A. should never be used for fastening sheet metal parts
    B. has two parallel threads running in the same direction
    C. has a right hand and a left hand thread
    D. can be used with a mating single-threaded nut

36. If the diameter of a circular piece of sheet metal is 11/2 feet, the area, in square inches,   36._____
is MOST NEARLY

    A. 1.77   B. 2.36   C. 254   D. 324

37. When removing a cartridge-type fuse from the fuse clips in a circuit, it is important to use   37._____
a fuse-puller PRIMARILY to avoid

    A. blowing the fuse   B. damaging the fuse
    C. arcing   D. personal injury

38. The MOST probable cause for the breaking of a drill bit while drilling into a steel plate is   38._____

    A. excessive drill pressure
    B. a hard spot in the steel
    C. a drill speed which is too low
    D. too much cutting-oil lubricant

39. In assembling structural steel, a drift pin is used to   39._____

    A. line up holes
    B. punch holes
    C. temporarily hold welded parts
    D. knock out structural bolts

40. The TIGHTEST fit for a mating shaft and hole is a _____ fit.   40._____

    A. running   B. sliding   C. working   D. force

KEY (CORRECT ANSWERS)

1.	C	11.	B	21.	C	31.	D
2.	A	12.	D	22.	A	32.	A
3.	C	13.	C	23.	B	33.	B
4.	D	14.	A	24.	D	34.	A
5.	A	15.	D	25.	D	35.	B
6.	D	16.	D	26.	C	36.	C
7.	A	17.	B	27.	D	37.	D
8.	A	18.	B	28.	B	38.	A
9.	B	19.	B	29.	C	39.	A
10.	C	20.	A	30.	C	40.	D

TEST 2

Each question or incomplete statement is followed by several suggested answers or completions. Select the one that BEST answers the question or completes the statement. *PRINT THE LETTER OF THE CORRECT ANSWER IN THE SPACE AT THE RIGHT.*

1. The crankshaft in a gasoline engine is PRIMARILY used to   1._____

    A.   change reciprocating motion to rotary motion
    B.   operate the valve lifters
    C.   supply power to each cylinder
    D.   function as a flywheel

2. Copper tubing is GENERALLY used in an annealed condition because annealing   2._____

    A.   gives the copper tubing a protective finish
    B.   makes the copper tubing harder
    C.   provides a smoother surface on the inner and outer walls
    D.   makes the copper tubing more ductile

3. Of the following, the MOST important advantage of a ratchet wrench as compared to an   3._____
   open-end wrench is that the ratchet wrench

    A.   is adjustable
    B.   cannot strip the threads of a nut
    C.   can be used in a limited space
    D.   measures the force applied

4. To provide a close-fitting hole for a taper pin, it is BEST to first drill the hole and then to   4._____
   use the appropriate

    A.   hone   B.   reamer
    C.   boring tool   D.   counterboring tool

5. If a part that is being checked for size fits loosely into a *NO-GO* gauge, it means that the   5._____

    A.   part is the proper size
    B.   part must be made smaller
    C.   part is the wrong size
    D.   gauge should be tightened

6. A hacksaw blade with 32 teeth per inch is BEST for cutting   6._____

    A.   materials less than 1/8-inch thick
    B.   a 3-inch diameter brass bar
    C.   1" thick copper plates
    D.   a 3-inch diameter steel bar

7. The BEST method to follow in order to prevent a drill from wandering upon starting to drill   7._____
   a hole in a steel plate is to

    A.   use a high-speed drill
    B.   first use a center-punch

C. use a drill with even cutting angles
D. exert heavy pressure when drilling

8. When grinding a tool, it is GOOD practice to keep moving the tool across the face of the grinding wheel in order to

8.____

A. prevent the tool from becoming too hot
B. avoid sparks
C. maintain a uniform grinding speed
D. prevent grooving the wheel

9. A material that is COMMONLY used as a lining for bearings in order to reduce friction is

9.____

A. magnesium
C. babbitt
B. cast iron
D. carborundum

10. In a motor having sleeve bearings, bearing wear can be checked by measuring the air-gap clearance between the armature and the

10.____

A. pole pieces
C. bearing
B. commutator
D. brushes

11. If the scale on a shop drawing is 1/4 inch to the foot, then the length of a part which measures 2 3/8 inches long on the drawing is ACTUALLY _____ feet.

11.____

A. 9 1/2 B. 8 1/2 C. 7 1/4 D. 4 1/4

12. When welding cast iron with an oxy-acetylene torch, the BEST weld is obtained when the cast iron is

12.____

A. not preheated
B. preheated slowly
C. chilled quickly after welding
D. chilled slowly after welding

13. A substance which can do the MOST damage to wire rope is

13.____

A. acid B. grease C. gasoline D. oil

14. When comparing the same nominal size of extra strong iron pipe with standard iron pipe, the extra strong iron pipe has _____ diameter _____ diameter.

14.____

A. the same inside; but a larger outside
B. the same outside; but a smaller inside
C. a larger outside; and a smaller inside
D. a larger inside; and a larger outside

15. A *Lally* column which is used in building construction consists of

15.____

A. a large diameter pipe fitted with a base plate at each end
B. channels tied with lattice bars
C. unequal sections of round pipe
D. angles and plates

16. On a 10-24 x 7/8" screw, the number 10 indicates that the size of the outside diameter is   16.____
MOST NEARLY

    A. 0.187"   B. 10/64"   C. 10/32"   D. 0.10"

17. The liquid solution in an electrical storage battery MOST commonly is   17.____

    A. alkali   B. acid
    C. pure distilled water   D. copper sulphate

18. Manifolds on an internal combustion engine are used   18.____

    A. to mount the engine to the frame
    B. for cooling the engine
    C. in the carburetor
    D. to conduct gases into and out of the engine

19. For winter servicing of a gasoline engine, it is BEST to use an oil that   19.____

    A. has a low SAE number
    B. has a high SAE number
    C. has a very heavy consistency
    D. contains few additive detergents

20. To remove a slotted collar having internal threads from a shaft, the BEST of the following   20.____
wrenches to use is a(n) _____ wrench.

    A. Allen   B. Stillson   C. socket   D. spanner

21. When using a heavy jack placed on the ground to raise a heavy load, it is important to   21.____
place a sturdy, flat board under the jack PRIMARILY in order to

    A. facilitate placing the jack under the load
    B. reduce the jacking effort
    C. prevent the jack from slipping out from under the load
    D. decrease the jacking height

22. The pulley wheels of a block and tackle are COMMONLY called   22.____

    A. stocks   B. swivels   C. sheaves   D. guides

23. If the diameter of a machined part must be 1.035 ± 0.003", then it is ACCEPTABLE if it   23.____
measures

    A. 1.031"   B. 1.032"   C. 1.039"   D. 1.335"

24. The type of threads for ordinary screws are USUALLY the _____ type.   24.____

    A. square   B. buttress   C. V   D. Acme

25. Lead is NORMALLY used in caulking _____ pipe.   25.____

    A. copper   B. brass
    C. steel   D. cast iron

26. Of the following materials, the one which is COMMONLY used as a lubricant is   26._____

     A. powdered iron oxide   B. powdered graphite
     C. casein   D. rosin flux

27. On grinders, the tool rest is generally 1/8-inch from the face of the wheel.   27._____
When dressing small parts on grinders, greater clearance is usually undesirable,
because too much clearance may cause

     A. the work piece to jam and break the wheel
     B. material from the work piece to be ground off too rapidly
     C. the cutting action of the grinder to be hidden from view
     D. scoring of the wheel

28. The BEST way to determine whether the locknuts on terminals in an electrical terminal   28._____
box have become loose is to

     A. use an electric tester
     B. try to tighten the nuts with an appropriate wrench
     C. tap the nuts with an insulated handle
     D. try to loosen the nuts with a pair of pliers

29. It is necessary to pour a new concrete floor for a shop. If the dimensions of the concrete   29._____
slab for the floor are to be 27' x 18' x 6", then the number of cubic yards of concrete that
must be poured is

     A. 9   B. 16   C. 54   D. 243

30. The jaws of a vise move 1/4" for each complete turn of the handle.   30._____
The number of complete turns necessary to open the jaws 2 3/4" is

     A. 9   B. 10   C. 11   D. 12

31. The sum of 5'6", 7'3", 9' 3 1/2", and 3' 7 1/4" is   31._____

     A. 19' 8 1/2"   B. 22' 1/2"   C. 25' 7 3/4"   D. 28' 8 3/4"

32. Of the following statements describing the use of carbon dioxide type fire extinguishers,   32._____
the one which is TRUE is that they

     A. may be used on grease fires
     B. should not be used to extinguish electrical fires
     C. can not be used on most types of fires
     D. are ideal for use in poorly ventilated areas

33. The PRIMARY reason for a twist drill *splitting up the center* is that the   33._____

     A. cutting edges were ground at different angles
     B. lips were ground at different lengths
     C. lip clearance angle was too great
     D. lip clearance angle was insufficient

34. The PROPER file a machinist should use for finishing ordinary flat surfaces is the _____   34._____
file.

     A. Pillar   B. Warding
     C. Hooktooth   D. Hand

35. An all hard saw blade should be used in a hacksaw frame when sawing 35.____

    A. tool steel   B. channel iron
    C. aluminum   D. thin wall copper tubing

36. The surface gage is generally NOT used for 36.____

    A. laying out
    B. leveling and lining up work
    C. checking angles and tapers
    D. locating centers on rough work

Questions 37-40.

DIRECTIONS: The sketch shown below refers to a piping arrangement for connecting a new space heater. Questions 37 through 40 are based on it.

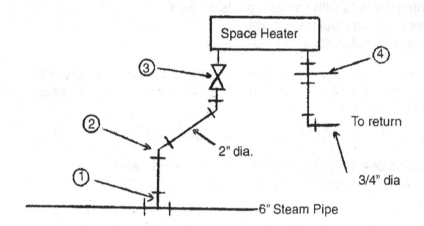

37. Pipe fitting 1 is a 37.____

    A. bull tee   B. sanitary tee
    C. reducing tee   D. cross

38. Pipe fitting 2 is a 38.____

    A. branch tee   B. Y fitting
    C. right elbow   D. 45 degree elbow

39. Pipe fitting 3 is a 39.____

    A. coupling   B. flange
    C. valve   D. steam trap

40. Pipe fitting 4 is a 40.____

    A. union   B. valve   C. tee   D. reducer

KEY (CORRECT ANSWERS)

1.	A	11.	A	21.	C	31.	C
2.	D	12.	B	22.	C	32.	A
3.	C	13.	A	23.	B	33.	D
4.	B	14.	B	24.	C	34.	D
5.	C	15.	A	25.	D	35.	A
6.	A	16.	A	26.	B	36.	C
7.	B	17.	B	27.	A	37.	C
8.	D	18.	D	28.	B	38.	D
9.	C	19.	A	29.	A	39.	C
10.	A	20.	D	30.	C	40.	A

———

EXAMINATION SECTION
TEST 1

DIRECTIONS: Each question or incomplete statement is followed by several suggested answers or completions. Select the one that BEST answers the question or completes the statement. *PRINT THE LETTER OF THE CORRECT ANSWER IN THE SPACE AT THE RIGHT.*

1. On an engine lathe, the saddle is a part which   1._____

    A.   is attached to the tailstock
    B.   rotates and holds the faceplate
    C.   slides along the ways
    D.   houses the back gears

2. To facilitate milling cast iron, it is BEST to use   2._____

    A.   an emulsion of soluble oil and water as a lubricant
    B.   an emulsion of soluble oil and water with a small percentage of soda as a lubricant
    C.   lard oil as a lubricant
    D.   no lubricant

3. When using a milling machine in a machine shop, a MAJOR difference of climb milling as compared to standard milling is that climb milling   3._____

    A.   uses more power
    B.   produces a better finish
    C.   uses a downward cut
    D.   uses cutters with less rake

4. In an automotive gasoline engine, the camshaft is used PRIMARILY to   4._____

    A.   drive the transmission
    B.   operate the valve lifters
    C.   change the reciprocating motion of the pistons to rotary motion
    D.   operate the choke mechanism

5. A magnetic motor starter is to be controlled with momentary start-stop pushbuttons at two locations.
The number of control wires required, respectively, in the conduit between the controller and the first station and in the conduit between the two stations is _____ and _____.   5._____

    A. 3;3   B. 4; 4   C. 3; 4   D. 2; 4

6. The type of fitting to use to join a 1 inch branch compressed air, pipe line to a 2 inch main air line is a   6._____

    A.   reducing valve   B.   reducing coupling
    C.   reducing tee   D.   street elbow

7. If steel weighs 0.30 pounds per cubic inch, then the weight of a 2 inch square steel bar 90 inches long is _____ pounds.   7._____

    A. 27   B. 54   C. 108   D. 360

8. In arc welding, the filler metal is provided PRIMARILY by   8._____

    A. the metal to be welded
    B. a second rod of filler metal
    C. the slag
    D. the electrode

9. Oil or grease should NOT be applied to the oxygen valve of an oxyacetylene torch PRI-   9._____
MARILY because this can

    A. produce an explosion hazard
    B. corrode the valve
    C. give an incorrect pressure reading
    D. make the valve too slippery to handle

10. The PRIMARY function of the thermostat in the cooling system of an automobile engine   10._____
is to

    A. control the operating temperature of the engine
    B. keep the operating temperature of the engine as low as possible
    C. provide the proper amount of heat for the heater
    D. retain engine heat when the engine gets hot

11. The PRIMARY purpose of the condenser in the ignition circuit of a gasoline engine is to   11._____

    A. boost the ignition voltage
    B. rectify the ignition voltage
    C. adjust the coil voltage
    D. reduce arcing at the distributor breaker points

12. The PRIMARY purpose of the differential in the rear drive train of an automotive vehicle   12._____
is to allow each of the rear wheels to

    A. rotate at different speeds
    B. go in reverse
    C. rotate with maximum torque
    D. absorb road shocks

13. When grinding a fillet weld smooth, it is best NOT to grind   13._____

    A. after the weld has cooled off
    B. slowly
    C. too much of the weld material away
    D. the surface smooth

14. When using a hand file to finish a round piece of wood rod held between lathe centers, it   14._____
is usually BEST to

    A. hold the file handle with one hand and to guide the file with the other hand
    B. use the file with the lathe not rotating
    C. hold the file with one hand and guide the workpiece with the other hand
    D. use a file without a handle

15. If the voltage on a 3-phase squirrel case induction motor is reduced to 90% of its rating, the starting current   15.____

    A. increases slightly   B. is unchanged
    C. decreases 10%   D. decreases 20%

16. If the voltage on a 3-phase squirrel case induction motor is reduced to 90% of its rating, the full load current   16.____

    A. decreases slightly   B. is unchanged
    C. increases 10%   D. increases 20%

17. When laying brick, the PRIMARY reason for wetting the brick before laying it is that   17.____

    A. the brick will absorb less water from the mortar and form a better bond
    B. wet bricks are easier to position
    C. wet bricks take less time to form a bond to mortar
    D. less cement is needed in the mortar

18. Concrete is a mixture that NORMALLY consists of cement,   18.____

    A. sand, and water   B. sand, mortar, and water
    C. gravel, and water   D. sand, gravel, and water

19. A type of rivet which can be put in place even when a worker does NOT have access to the back side of the work is known as a _____ rivet.   19.____

    A. *bucking*   B. *double-head*
    C. *pop*   D. *side*

20. The fraction which is equal to 0.875 is   20.____

    A. 7/16   B. 5/8   C. 3/4   D. 7/8

21. When fabricating forms for pouring concrete, the MAIN advantage of using plywood sheets over sheets made of pine boards is that plywood   21.____

    A. doesn't splinter   B. is lighter
    C. is less expensive   D. resists warping better

22. When chipping concrete with a pneumatic hammer, the MOST important safety item that a man should wear is   22.____

    A. goggles   B. gloves
    C. a hard hat   D. rubber boots

23. It is considered POOR practice to paint a wooden ladder PRIMARILY because the   23.____

    A. paint will wear off in time
    B. rails will become susceptible to damage
    C. paint will shorten the life of the rungs
    D. paint can hide serious defects

24. A concrete wall is 36' long, 9' high, and 1 1/2' thick. The number of cubic yards of concrete that were needed to make this wall is   24.____

    A. 14   B. 18   C. 27   D. 36

25. Before disassembling a complex mechanical machine, a mechanic may use a center punch to make adjacent punch marks on two or more of the parts in the machine in order to

    A. mark each part as he removes it
    B. check the hardness of the parts
    C. loosen the parts
    D. give himself a guide for correct reassembly

25.____

26. From among the following tools, the BEST one to use in cutting off a section of 4-inch cast iron pipe would be a

    A. hammer and chisel   B. pneumatic hammer
    C. hammer and star drill   D. hacksaw

26.____

27. The MOST important reason for removing pressure from an air hose before breaking a hose connection is to avoid

    A. damage to the air compressor
    B. losing air
    C. damage to the hose connection
    D. personal injury

27.____

28. When using a rope fall to lower a heavy load vertically, the strain on the hand line can be reduced and the load lowered more safely if the

    A. rope is wound three or four times around a fixed post
    B. rope is lightly greased
    C. rope is held very tightly in the sheaves of the fall
    D. sheaves of the fall are small in diameter

28.____

29. Oil is frequently applied to the inside of forms prior to pouring concrete in them in order to

    A. make the concrete flow better
    B. make stripping easier
    C. keep the moisture in the concrete
    D. protect the forms

29.____

30. The instrument generally used to determine the specific gravity of a lead-acid storage battery is the

    A. ammeter   B. voltmeter   C. ohmmeter   D. hydrometer

30.____

31. A tachometer is an instrument that is used to measure

    A. horizontal distances
    B. radial distances
    C. current in electric circuits
    D. motor speed

31.____

32. If the centers of a lathe are out of line when turning a cylindrical piece, it will cause

    A. the centers to be damaged
    B. a spiral groove to be cut on the piece

32.____

C.   the cutting tool to be damaged
D.   the piece to have a taper

33.   A low reading on the oil pressure gauge of a gasoline engine may mean that the   33.____

A.   engine bearings are too tight
B.   crankcase oil level is too low
C.   transmission oil level is too low
D.   transmission oil needs changing

34.   Although cloth tapes are used for taking measurements in many kinds of work, they   34.____
should NOT be used when taking accurate measurements PRIMARILY because

A.   small changes in the amount of pull on these tapes can make a big difference in
the reading
B.   the numbers become worn easily and are thus difficult to read
C.   small temperature changes cause large changes in readings
D.   there are too few subdivisions of each inch on these tapes

35.   When painting walls with two coats of paint, a different color is used for each coat PRI-   35.____
MARILY to

A.   check for full coverage by the second coat
B.   provide a better appearance
C.   lower the painting cost
D.   allow the painter to use any color paint for the first coat

36.   To drill a hole in the same place on a number of identical steel parts, it is BEST to use a   36.____

A.   blanking tool   B.   punch press
C.   counterbore   D.   jig

37.   The MAIN purpose of a chuck on a lathe is to   37.____

A.   hold the workpiece
B.   hold the cutting tool
C.   allow speed changes to be made
D.   allow screw threads to be turned

38.   The metal which has the GREATEST resistance to the flow of electricity is   38.____

A.   steel   B.   copper   C.   silver   D.   gold

39.   Tinning a soldering iron means   39.____

A.   applying flux to the tip
B.   cleaning the tip to make it bright
C.   applying a coat of solder to the tip
D.   heating the iron to the proper temperature

40. A protractor is an instrument that is used to

    A. measure the thickness of shims
    B. drill blind holes
    C. measure angles
    D. drill tapped holes

40.____

KEY (CORRECT ANSWERS)

1.	C	11.	D	21.	D	31.	D
2.	D	12.	A	22.	A	32.	D
3.	C	13.	C	23.	D	33.	B
4.	B	14.	A	24.	B	34.	A
5.	C	15.	C	25.	D	35.	A
6.	C	16.	C	26.	A	36.	D
7.	C	17.	A	27.	D	37.	A
8.	D	18.	D	28.	A	38.	A
9.	A	19.	C	29.	B	39.	C
10.	A	20.	D	30.	D	40.	C

TEST 2

DIRECTIONS: Each question or incomplete statement is followed by several suggested answers or completions. Select the one that BEST answers the question or completes the statement. *PRINT THE LETTER OF THE CORRECT ANSWER IN THE SPACE AT THE RIGHT.*

1. Common nail sizes are designated by   1.____

    A. penny size   B. weight
    C. head size   D. shank diameter

2. Toggle bolts should be used to fasten conduit clamps to a _____ wall.   2.____

    A. concrete   B. hollow tile
    C. brick   D. solid masonry

3. Backlash in a pair of meshed gears is defined as the   3.____

    A. distance between the gear centers
    B. gear ratio of the pair
    C. wear of the teeth
    D. *play* between the gear teeth

4. Relief valves on an air supply reservoir are used for the purpose of   4.____

    A. protecting the reservoir against excessively high pressures
    B. compensating for air leakage from the reservoir
    C. retaining the air in the reservoir
    D. draining moisture from the reservoir

5. Of the following, the BEST tool to use for securely tightening a one-inch standard hexag-   5.____
onal nut is a(n)

    A. monkey wrench   B. open-end wrench
    C. Stillson wrench   D. pair of heavy duty pliers

6. The type of pipe which is MOST likely to be broken by careless handling is one made of   6.____

    A. copper   B. steel   C. brass   D. cast iron

7. Open-end wrenches are usually made with the sides of the jaws at about a 15 degree   7.____
angle to the centerline of the handle.
The PURPOSE of this type of design is that it

    A. increases the leverage of the wrench
    B. enables the wrench to lock on to the bolt head
    C. is useful when using the wrench in close quarters
    D. prevents extending the handle with a piece of pipe

8. The type of tool which is used with a portable electric drill to cut 2-inch diameter circular   8.____
holes in wood is the

    A. reamer   B. twist drill
    C. hole saw   D. circular saw

9. For a certain job, you will need 25 steel bars 1 inch in diameter and 4'6" long. If these bars weigh 3 pounds per foot of length, then the TOTAL weight for all 25 bars is _____ pounds.

   A. 13.5   B. 75.0   C. 112.5   D. 337.5

9.___

10. If the allowable load on a wooden scaffold is 60 pounds per square foot and the scaffold surface area is 3 feet by 12 feet, then the MAXIMUM total distributed load that is permitted on the scaffold is _____ pounds.

   A. 720   B. 1800   C. 2160   D. 2400

10.___

11. If the floor area of one shop is 15' by 21'3" and the size of an adjacent shop is 18' by 30'6", then the TOTAL floor area of these two shops is _____ square feet.

   A. 1127.75   B. 867.75   C. 549.0   D. 318.75

11.___

12. To make certain that two points separated by a vertical distance of 8 feet are in exact vertical alignment, it would be BEST to use a

   A. plumb bob   B. spirit level
   C. protractor   D. mason's line

12.___

13. An offset screwdriver is MOST useful for turning a wood screw when

   A. the screw is large
   B. space above the screw is limited
   C. the screw is the Phillips type
   D. the screw must be tightened very securely

13.___

14. If an 8-32 x 11" machine screw is not available, the screw which could MOST easily be modified to use in an emergency is the

   A. 8-36 x 1"   B. 10-32 x 1"
   C. 6-32 x 1 1/2"   D. 8-32 x 1 1/2"

14.___

15. After a file has been used on soft material, the BEST way to clean the file is to use

   A. a file card   B. fine emery cloth
   C. a bench brush   D. a cleaning solution

15.___

16. The type of wrench that should be used to tighten a nut or bolt to a specified number of foot-pounds is a _____ wrench.

   A. torque   B. spanner   C. box   D. lug

16.___

17. When a hacksaw blade is turned at right angles to its holding frame, it is done PRIMARILY to

   A. increase the accuracy of cutting
   B. reduce the strain on the frame
   C. cut more rapidly
   D. make cuts which are deeper than the frame

17.___

18. The PRIMARY purpose of galvanizing steel is to

   A. increase the strength of the steel
   B. provide a good base for painting

18.___

C. prevent rusting of the steel
D. improve the appearance of the steel

19. When installing a heavy new machine in a shop, the BEST way to level the machine on the shop floor is to

19.____

A. use steel shims under the feet
B. use a thin layer of cement under the feet
C. grind the feet of the machine to suit
D. install adjustable shock mounts

20. The type of valve that permits fluid to flow in one direction ONLY in a pipe run is a _____ valve.

20.____

A. check   B. gate   C. globe   D. cross

21. If the scale on a shop drawing is 1/2 inch to the foot, then the length of a part which measures 4 1/4 inches long on the drawing has a length of APPROXIMATELY _____ feet.

21.____

A. 2 1/8   B. 4 1/4   C. 8 1/2   D. 10 3/4

22. It is important to use safety shoes PRIMARILY to guard the feet against

22.____

A. tripping hazards   B. heavy falling objects
C. shock hazards   D. mud and dirt

23. When using a wrench to tighten a bolt, it is considered BAD practice to extend the handle of the wrench with a pipe for added leverage PRIMARILY because

23.____

A. the pipe may break
B. the bolt head may be broken off
C. more space will be needed to turn the wrench with the pipe on it
D. no increase in leverage is obtained in this manner

24. To accurately measure the small gap between relay contacts, it is BEST to use a(n)

24.____

A. depth gauge   B. GO-NO GO gauge
C. feeler gauge   D. inside caliper

25. The plumbing symbol shown on the right represents a
A. steam trap
B. coupling
C. cross fitting
D. valve

25.____

26. On oxyacetylene welding equipment, the feed pressure of the gases is reduced by means of

26.____

A. tip valves   B. regulator valves
C. relief valves   D. nozzle size

27. The purpose of the ignition coil in a gasoline engine is PRIMARILY to

27.____

A. smooth the voltage   B. raise the voltage
C. raise the current   D. smooth the current

33

28. The weight per foot of length of a 2" x 2" square steel bar as compared to a 1" x 1" square steel bar is _____ times as much.

    A. two   B. four   C. six   D. eight

28.____

29. Electric arc welding is COMMONLY done using _____ amperage and _____ voltage.

    A. low; low   B. low; high
    C. high; low   D. high; high

29.____

30. Creosote is COMMONLY used

    A. to preserve wood
    B. to produce a good finish on wood
    C. as a primer coat of paint on wood
    D. to fireproof wood

30.____

31. The term *shipping* when applied to rope means

    A. coiling the rope in a tight ball
    B. lubricating the strands with tallow
    C. wetting the rope with water to make it easier to coil
    D. binding the ends with cord to prevent unraveling

31.____

32. Many portable electric power tools, such as electric drills, which operate on 110V A.C., have a third conductor in the power cord.
The reason for this extra conductor is to

    A. prevent overheating of the power cord
    B. provide a spare conductor
    C. make the power cord stronger
    D. ground the case of the tool

32.____

33. The sum of 4 feet 3 1/4 inches, 7 feet 2 1/2 inches, and 11 feet 1/4 inch is _____ feet _____ inches.

    A. 21; 6 1/4   B. 22; 6   C. 23; 5   D. 24; 5 3/4

33.____

34. The number 0.038 is read as

    A. 38 tenths   B. 38 hundredths
    C. 38 thousandths   D. 38 ten-thousandths

34.____

35. Assume that an employee is paid at the rate of $5.43 per hour with time and a half for overtime past 40 hours in a week.
If he works 43 hours in a week, his gross weekly pay is

    A. $217.20   B. $219.20   C. $229.59   D. $241.64

35.____

36. Vapor lock in a vehicle with a gasoline engine is caused by excessive heat.
To prevent vapor lock, it may be necessary to relocate the(a)

    A. ignition system   B. cooling system
    C. starter motor   D. part of the fuel line

36.____

37. An ohmmeter is an instrument for measuring electrical

    A. voltage   B. current   C. power   D. resistance

37.____

38. A thermal overload device on a motor is used to protect it against 38.____

    A. high voltage
    B. over-speeding
    C. excessively high current
    D. low temperatures

39. A union is a pipe fitting that is used to join together 39.____

    A. two pipes of different diameters
    B. two pipes of the same diameter
    C. a threaded pipe to a sweated pipe
    D. two sweated pipes of the same diameter

40. If a 30 ampere fuse is placed in a fuse box for a circuit requiring a 15 ampere fuse, 40.____

    A. serious damage to the circuit may result from an overload
    B. better protection will be provided for the circuit
    C. the larger fuse will tend to blow more often since it carries more current
    D. it will eliminate maintenance problems

―――――

KEY (CORRECT ANSWERS)

1.	A	11.	B	21.	C	31.	D
2.	B	12.	A	22.	B	32.	D
3.	D	13.	B	23.	B	33.	B
4.	A	14.	D	24.	C	34.	C
5.	B	15.	A	25.	D	35.	D
6.	D	16.	A	26.	B	36.	D
7.	C	17.	D	27.	B	37.	D
8.	C	18.	C	28.	B	38.	C
9.	D	19.	A	29.	C	39.	B
10.	C	20.	A	30.	A	40.	A

―――――

35

EXAMINATION SECTION
TEST 1

DIRECTIONS: Each question consists of a statement. You are to indicate whether the statement is TRUE (T) or FALSE (F). *PRINT THE LETTER OF THE CORRECT ANSWER IN THE SPACE AT THE RIGHT.*

1. One square foot is equal to 144 square inches.   1.____

2. One cubic foot of water weighs APPROXIMATELY 8 1/2 pounds.   2.____

3. One bag of portland cement weighs APPROXIMATELY 94 pounds.   3.____

4. If a board foot is 12 inches by 12 inches by one inch, the number of board feet in a plank 18 feet long, 10 inches wide, 4 inches thick is 360.   4.____

5. If a cubic foot of water contains 7 1/2 gallons, the number of gallons contained in a tank 6 feet long, 4 feet wide, and 2 feet deep is 360.   5.____

6. The total surface area of a 6 inch solid cube is 144 square inches.   6.____

7. 1728 cubic feet equal 192 cubic yards.   7.____

8. When the mix proportion for a concrete sidewalk is given as 1:3:5, the numbers give the ratio by volume of cement to sand to coarse aggregate.   8.____

9. When oily waste rags are not in use, it is good practice to store them in self-closing metal containers.   9.____

10. The CHIEF purpose of a trap under a plumbing fixture is to act as a seal against sewer gas.   10.____

11. If a rectangular frame measures 12 inches long and 9 inches wide, the length of its diagonal is 21 inches.   11.____

12. Threads on the inside of metal pipes are usually cut with dies.   12.____

13. A screwdriver is the proper tool to drive a lag screw into place.   13.____

14. The diameter of one inch pipe is measured from the outside of the pipe.   14.____

15. If the counterweights of the top sash of a window are too heavy, more exertion will be necessary to close that half of the window.   15.____

16. Glazed tile should be wet prior to being laid.   16.____

17. The striking plate is part of a lockset.   17.____

18. A casement window usually slides up and down.   18.____

19. An escutcheon plate is part of a lockset.   19.____

20. When using a hand saw, it is good practice to pull up rather than push down the saw when starting the first stroke.   20.____

21. Hickory is a very brittle wood.   21._____

22. Timber which is continually wet will not rot as soon as timber which is alternately wet and   22._____
dry.

23. A nosing is the projecting edge of a stair tread.   23._____

24. When sawing wood marked off with a pencil line, the saw should be driven through the   24._____
center of the pencil line.

25. One 45 degree elbow fitting will make a right angle.   25._____

26. The MOST probable cause of the water of a flush tank of a toilet continuing to flow after   26._____
the flushing has stopped is that the rubber ball fails to seat properly.

27. Nails driven with the grain of the wood do not hold as well as when driven across the   27._____
grain.

28. Usually sandpapering of wood should be done with the grain.   28._____

29. After concrete sidewalks are poured in the open air, they are usually covered with straw   29._____
or paper in order to give a bright color to the sidewalk.

30. To prevent screws from splitting the wood when they are being driven, it is good practice   30._____
to drill a small hole first.

31. The PRINCIPAL purpose of a leader is to carry away sewage from a building.   31._____

32. The PRINCIPAL purpose of a hacksaw is to cut thin wood.   32._____

33. The board around a room at the bottom of the walls is known as a baseboard.   33._____

34. Clay tiles, when used on the interior of buildings, are usually set in Portland cement mor-   34._____
tar.

35. Before window glass is set in wooden window sashes, putty should be placed in the   35._____
rebates of the sash.

36. Clear window glass is made in ONLY one thickness.   36._____

37. Glass which is to be set in wooden sash windows should be cut to the exact measure-   37._____
ments between the sashes.

38. Three eighths (3/8") of an inch is equivalent to .0375".   38._____

39. Nipples are short pieces of pipe threaded only on one end.   39._____

40. Pipe fittings which connect pipes so that they may be at an angle to each other are   40._____
known as elbows.

41. Solder is a mixture of lead and brass.   41._____

42. A yellow flame in the burner of a gas range usually indicates that the proper amount of   42._____
air for combustion is present.

43. Gaskets are generally used to relieve clogged drain pipes. 43.____

44. The PRINCIPAL purpose of galvanizing iron is to prevent rust. 44.____

45. When driving a long nail into a piece of wood, it is good practice to start hammering with light blows. 45.____

46. If a maintenance man is to remove a door having two hinges from its frame, he should FIRST remove the lower hinge. 46.____

47. If a 10 ampere fuse blows out constantly, it should be replaced with a 15 ampere fuse. 47.____

48. When grinding a tool, the stone should revolve towards the bevel edge of the tool that is pressed against it. 48.____

49. The upright members of a wooden door are known as rails. 49.____

50. Casement windows are balanced with weights. 50.____

———

KEY (CORRECT ANSWERS)

1.	T	11.	F	21.	F	31.	F	41.	F
2.	F	12.	F	22.	T	32.	F	42.	F
3.	T	13.	F	23.	T	33.	T	43.	F
4.	F	14.	F	24.	F	34.	T	44.	T
5.	T	15.	F	25.	F	35.	T	45.	T
6.	F	16.	T	26.	T	36.	F	46.	T
7.	F	17.	T	27.	T	37.	F	47.	F
8.	T	18.	F	28.	T	38.	F	48.	T
9.	T	19.	T	29.	F	39.	F	49.	F
10.	T	20.	T	30.	T	40.	T	50.	F

———

TEST 2

DIRECTIONS: Each question consists of a statement. You are to indicate whether the statement is TRUE (T) or FALSE (F). *PRINT THE LETTER OF THE CORRECT ANSWER IN THE SPACE AT THE RIGHT.*

1. Stillson wrench is another name for a monkey wrench.   1.____

2. To draw a nail from a board with a claw hammer, the greatest drawing power will result when the handle of the hammer is held at the end farthest from the head.   2.____

3. To remove paint spots from a wooden desk, it is BETTER to use turpentine rather than linseed oil.   3.____

4. The water level in the flushing tank of a water closet should not be lower than the overflow opening,   4.____

5. The BEST method of repairing cracks in a toilet bowl of solid porcelain is to putty them.   5.____

6. When making concrete by hand, the sand and cement should be nixed together before adding water.   6.____

7. To lift a heavy object from the floor, a person should keep the legs straight and do the lifting with his back.   7.____

8. It is not good practice to report accidents on a job when they do not seem to be serious.   8.____

9. Tools used by workmen should generally be cleaned before storing away each night.   9.____

10. If a maintenance man receives an order from his foreman to do a job which he does not understand, he should use his own judgment and go ahead with the job.   10.____

11. The legs of a compass should be spread 5 inches apart in order to draw a circle with a diameter 5 inches.   11.____

12. A box measuring 18 inches square and 16 inches deep will have a volume of 36 cubic feet.   12.____

13. When setting glass in windows, it is good practice to give the wood a coat of linseed oil before applying the putty.   13.____

14. A nail set is used to drive wood screws beneath the surface of the floor.   14.____

15. When replacing a door in its frame, the top hinge should be attached before the bottom hinge.   15.____

16. A ripsaw is the proper tool for cutting metal pipe.   16.____

17. In cold weather the temperature of a room may be lowered due to conduction of heat through window glass.   17.____

18. The object of marking off sidewalks into rectangular slabs is to prevent pedestrians slipping on the completed walk.   18.____

19. The CHIEF purpose in keeping tools and supplies in orderly manner is to discourage theft of the tools.　　19.____

20. The horizontal members of a wooden door are known as rails.　　20.____

21. A wood chisel is sharpened only on one side.　　21.____

22. A screwdriver is the proper tool for driving a nail below the surface of the wood.　　22.____

23. Putty for window glazing is usually made of cement and linseed oil.　　23.____

24. Hickory is a suitable wood for handles of hammers.　　24.____

25. The number on the saw blade of a carpenter's saw near the handle indicates the width of the saw at the point.　　25.____

26. The vertical part of stair steps is called the riser.　　26.____

27. A reamer is the CORRECT tool with which to put threads on a pipe.　　27.____

28. A person should face the ladder as he descends on it.　　28.____

29. A center punch is used for marking points on metal at which holes are to be drilled.　　29.____

30. A stud bolt has a square head.　　30.____

31. The teeth of saws are usually bent sideways alternately to prevent saw binding in the cut slot.　　31.____

32. When inserting a pane of window glass in a wooden window sash, glazier's points should be forced into the sash after the puttying has been completed.　　32.____

33. Lead poisoning may result after eating meals while red lead or lead filings are under the nails of the hands of the worker.　　33.____

34. A coupling is a pipe fitting with internal threads.　　34.____

35. A tee joint for pipe has 3 openings.　　35.____

36. A die is generally used to cut threads in a nut.　　36.____

37. Glass is a good electrical conductor.　　37.____

38. Small nails used in fine work are called rivets.　　38.____

39. A fuse wire should melt less readily than the wiring in the circuit which it protects.　　39.____

40. The diameter of a circle is equal to half its circumference.　　40.____

41. The unit of electrical resistance is the ampere.　　41.____

42. Where only a short swing of the handle is possible, the ratchet type wrench is best used.　　42.____

43. Iron coated with tin is called galvanized iron.　　43.____

44. An advantage of cast iron is that it bends very easily but does not break.　　44.____

45. Monel metal rusts very quickly.   45._____

46. A *compass* saw is best used for cutting heavy boards.   46._____

47. Brads are used to fasten heavy boards together.   47._____

48. When used in connection with nails, *penny* refers to quality.   48._____

49. An expansion bolt is usually used to allow for expansion and contraction due to climatic   49._____
    conditions.

50. The French polish finish is the FINEST shellac finish that there is.   50._____

KEY (CORRECT ANSWERS)

1. F	11. F	21. T	31. T	41. F
2. T	12. F	22. F	32. F	42. T
3. T	13. T	23. F	33. T	43. F
4. F	14. F	24. T	34. T	44. F
5. F	15. T	25. F	35. T	45. F
6. T	16. F	26. T	36. F	46. F
7. F	17. T	27. F	37. T	47. F
8. F	18. F	28. T	38. F	48. F
9. T	19. F	29. T	39. F	49. F
10. F	20. T	30. F	40. F	50. T

TEST 3

DIRECTIONS: Each question consists of a statement. You are to indicate whether the statement is TRUE (T) or FALSE (F). *PRINT THE LETTER OF THE CORRECT ANSWER IN THE SPACE AT THE RIGHT.*

1.   To lay out very precise work on wood, it is BEST to use a chalk line.   1._____

2.   A ripsaw is BEST used for cutting wood across the grain.   2._____

3.   Beach sand, because of its uniform grain, will make a dense and strong concrete.   3._____

4.   A *union* is the same as a *coupling* in plumbing.   4._____

5.   A valve that permits free passage of water through a pipe or valve in one direction, but prevents a reversal of flow, is called a check valve.   5._____

6.   Iron or steel fittings used with brass or copper pipe would cause an electrical action that would be unsatisfactory.   6._____

7.   Brass and copper are USUALLY softer than iron or steel.   7._____

8.   While pipe is being cut to length and threaded, it is held securely in place usually by a pipe vise.   8._____

9.   With respect to water closets, pressure flush valves are usually used without a tank.   9._____

10. Troubles resulting from low velocity of liquids flowing through horizontal pipes are greatly lessened by giving these pipes a downward pitch toward the soil.   10._____

11. Water is delivered to the building under pressure from a street main.
     The pipe coming into the building is usually called the downtake pipe.   11._____

12. Elbows usually have female threads at both ends.   12._____

13. Extensive tests have shown that the strength of timber is increased as its moisture content is decreased.   13._____

14. Thawing a frozen water pipe by means of a blowtorch is highly recommended.   14._____

15. Heat applied to a frozen water pipe should be applied first at the middle of the frozen part.   15._____

16. Water closet traps may be cleaned with a tool called a closet auger.
     This is usually operated by compressed air.   16._____

17. With respect to faucet washers, leather and fibre washers are satisfactory for cold water, but composition materials generally last longer on the hot water side.   17._____

18. A pipe cutter leaves a larger burr on the outside of a pipe than on the inside.   18._____

19. In threading pipe, dirt and chips in the stock and die will result in imperfect threads.   19._____

20. The burr resulting from cutting pipe is BEST removed by a pipe tapper.   20._____

21. With respect to pipe, the abbreviation I.P.S. means iron pipe shape. 21.____

22. Caustic potash when used as a drain pipe solvent will NOT damage aluminum. 22.____

23. Any pipe which carries the discharge from one or more water closets to the house drain is called a soil pipe. 23.____

24. A vent stack is a vertical pipe whose primary purpose is to allow circulation of air to and from any other piping in the drainage system of the building. 24.____

25. Evaporation may gradually reduce the depth of trap water in case a fixture remains unused for long periods. 25.____

26. The rubber ball stopper in a flush tank is held in place normally by air pressure. 26.____

27. In water closets an overflow tube allows water to flow into the closet bowl should the ball cock fail to close and the level rises too high in the tank. 27.____

28. When the ground seat in a compression faucet has become pitted or grooved, the seat should be dressed down true with a reamer. 28.____

29. A chamfer is a kind of bevel. 29.____

30. A corrugated fastener for joining two pieces of wood can sometimes be used in place of a nail.
It should be driven by heavy blows from a heavy hammer. 30.____

31. No. 1 sandpaper is finer than number 4 sandpaper. 31.____

32. To *rod* a sewer pipe means to support the sewer pipe with reinforcing metal rods. 32.____

33. *T* and *G*, when applied to lumber, means tested and guaranteed. 33.____

34. When a screwdriver is used on a small object, the object should be held in the palm of the hand. 34.____

35. An oval faced hammer is BEST for driving nails. 35.____

36. Metal sash chains are usually of the flat link type. 36.____

37. A casement window can swing only one way, and that way is out. 37.____

38. The mark *UL* on electrical equipment usually means universal license. 38.____

39. Every door closing or checking device must be mounted overhead on the door. 39.____

40. A wash basin with a pop up drain always has a stopper and chain. 40.____

41. A fusible plug is usually used to make a temporary repair on a leaking water pipe. 41.____

42. To be effective, a thermostat must always have a clock connected with it. 42.____

43. Wood with narrow annual rings is denser and stronger than wood with wide annual rings. 43.____

44. BX in the electrical industry means best grade. 44.____

45. A sub-metering device means a device usually buried and underground in the street. 45.____

46. An oscillating fan is designed to run faster automatically as the room temperature rises. 46.____

47. An electrical cooking stove requires a *booster* to light a burner. 47.____

48. A universal motor is designed to operate with either A.C. or D.C. power. 48.____

49. An A.C. fuse will NOT operate on D.C. 49.____

50. Special circuit wiring is required for the installation of fluorescent lighting fixtures. 50.____

KEY (CORRECT ANSWERS)

1.	F	11.	F	21.	F	31.	T	41.	F
2.	F	12.	T	22.	F	32.	F	42.	F
3.	F	13.	T	23.	T	33.	F	43.	T
4.	F	14.	F	24.	T	34.	F	44.	F
5.	T	15.	F	25.	T	35.	F	45.	F
6.	T	16.	F	26.	F	36.	T	46.	F
7.	T	17.	T	27.	T	37.	F	47.	F
8.	T	18.	F	28.	F	38.	F	48.	T
9.	T	19.	T	29.	T	39.	F	49.	F
10.	T	20.	F	30.	F	40.	F	50.	F

TEST 4

DIRECTIONS: Each question consists of a statement. You are to indicate whether the statement is TRUE (T) or FALSE (F). *PRINT THE LETTER OF THE CORRECT ANSWER IN THE SPACE AT THE RIGHT.*

1. *Scotch* tape is preferable to friction tape for the splicing of electrical conductors. 1.____

2. With respect to passenger elevators, car doors and shaft doors are the same. 2.____

3. A pendant fixture is a fixture hanging or suspended. 3.____

4. A rectifier changes A.C. to D.C. current. 4.____

5. A knife switch is used to cut small sections of wire from a spool of wire. 5.____

6. Domestic electric bills are usually rendered for kilowatt hours consumed. 6.____

7. When lamps are connected in series, if one goes out, all go out. 7.____

8. A household iron usually consumes about 110 watts. 8.____

9. The dry cell battery supplies alternating current. 9.____

10. On the dry cell battery, one terminal is called the positive and the other is called the negative. 10.____

11. An annunciator is a device to change the voltage of a current of electricity. 11.____

12. The average household electric bulb contains air under heavy pressure. 12.____

13. Insulators offer high resistance to the flow of electricity. 13.____

14. The smaller the wire, the larger the current carrying capacity of the wire. 14.____

15. #14 wire is smaller than #8 wire. 15.____

16. Transformers can operate only on A.C. 16.____

17. Some cartridge fuses are renewable by replacing the fuse element. 17.____

18. A *short* in a circuit should *blow* the fuse. 18.____

19. A circuit breaker is a type of conduit. 19.____

20. A miter box is used to store small nails, washers, and tools on the job. 20.____

21. When a hidden edge is shown on a drawing, it is represented by a dotted line. 21.____

22. A rasp is a kind of heavy hammer. 22.____

23. *Green* lumber is lumber not well seasoned. 23.____

24. A dowel is usually triangular in shape. 24.____

25. Monkey wrenches usually have jaws with teeth. 25.____

26. The only material that can cut glass is a diamond, or diamond chip.   26._____

27. An extension ladder and a step ladder are the same.   27._____

28. A turnbuckle is a type of general purpose wrench.   28._____

29. Terrazzo is a kind of concealed joint used in expensive cabinet work.   29._____

30. A burr is a kind of metal measuring tape.   30._____

31. Armored cable is cable with a soft outer covering but with very heavy inside wire.   31._____

32. Continued use of a portable electric room heater will *use up* the oxygen in a small closed room quicker than a gas heater.   32._____

33. Plate glass is generally superior to sheet glass for windows.   33._____

34. White pine is a harder wood than white oak.   34._____

35. Chestnut is usually considered an *open grained* wood.   35._____

36. #30 sheet iron is thicker than #14.   36._____

37. Semi-vitreous tiles are generally harder than vitreous tiles.   37._____

38. One disadvantage of interlocking rubber tiling is that it is *noisy* in use.   38._____

39. A *light* of glass is the same as a *pane* of glass.   39._____

40. The scratch coat of plaster is the last coat to be applied.   40._____

41. The riser pipe in a heating system is usually horizontal.   41._____

42. With reference to wire specifications, AWG means American Wire Gage.   42._____

43. Electric motors are never rated in terms of horsepower.   43._____

44. The use of self-closing water faucets should help reduce water waste.   44._____

45. *Push button* elevators are manufactured only by the Otis Elevator Company.   45._____

46. Gas bills are usually computed on the basis of cubic feet consumed.   46._____

47. With respect to pipe, I.D. usually means inside diameter.   47._____

48. Graphite is sometimes used as a lubricant.   48._____

49. A blow torch can burn gasoline only.   49._____

50. Bronze is composed CHIEFLY of copper and tin.   50._____

———

KEY (CORRECT ANSWERS)

1.	F	11.	F	21.	T	31.	F	41.	F
2.	F	12.	F	22.	F	32.	F	42.	T
3.	T	13.	T	23.	T	33.	T	43.	F
4.	T	14.	F	24.	F	34.	F	44.	T
5.	F	15.	T	25.	F	35.	T	45.	F
6.	T	16.	T	26.	F	36.	F	46.	T
7.	T	17.	T	27.	F	37.	F	47.	T
8.	F	18.	T	28.	F	38.	F	48.	T
9.	F	19.	F	29.	F	39.	T	49.	F
10.	T	20.	F	30.	F	40.	F	50.	T

———

EXAMINATION SECTION
TEST 1

DIRECTIONS: Each question or incomplete statement is followed by several suggested answers or completions. Select the one that BEST answers the question or completes the statement. *PRINT THE LETTER OF THE CORRECT ANSWER IN THE SPACE AT THE RIGHT.*

1.

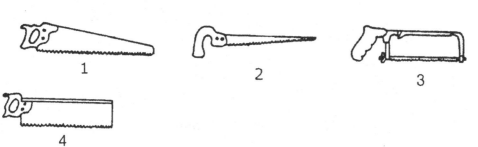

The saw that is used PRINCIPALLY where curved cuts are to be made is numbered

   A. 1   B. 2   C. 3   D. 4

1.____

2.

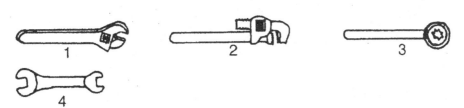

The wrench that is used PRINCIPALLY for pipe work is numbered

   A. 1   B. 2   C. 3   D. 4

2.____

3.

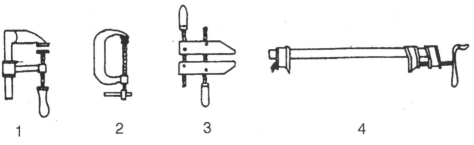

The carpenter's *hand screw* is numbered

   A. 1   B. 2   C. 3   D. 4

3.____

4.

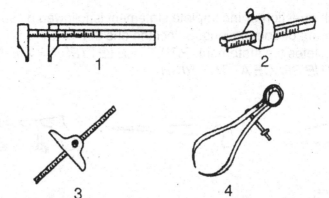

1

2

3

4

The tool used to measure the depth of a hole is numbered

A. 1   B. 2   C. 3   D. 4

5.

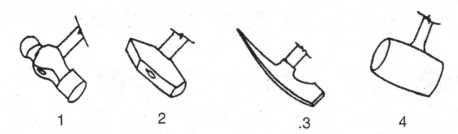

1   2   .3   4

The tool that is BEST suited for use with a wood chisel is numbered

A. 1   B. 2   C. 3   D. 4

6.

1   2   3   4

The screw head that would be tightened with an *Allen* wrench is numbered

A. 1   B. 2   C. 3   D. 4

7.

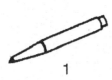   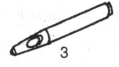

1   2   3

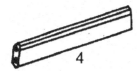

4

The center punch is numbered

A. 1   B. 2   C. 3   D. 4

8.

1

2

3

4

The tool used to drill a hole in concrete is numbered

A. 1   B. 2   C. 3   D. 4

8.____

9.

1

2

3

4

The wrench whose PRINCIPAL purpose to to hold taps for threading is numbered

A. 1   B. 2   C. 3   D. 4

9.____

10.

1

2

3

4

The electrician's bit is indicated by the number

A. 1   B. 2   C. 3   D. 4

10.____

11. The ends of a joist in a brick building are cut to a bevel. This is done PRINCIPALLY to prevent damage to

A. joist   B. floor   C. sill   D. wall

11.____

12. Of the following, the wood that is MOST commonly used today for floor joists is   12.____

   A. long leaf yellow pine   B. douglas fir
   C. oak   D. birch

13. Quarter-sawed lumber is preferred for the BEST finished flooring PRINCIPALLY because   13.____
it

   A. has the greatest strength   B. shrinks the least
   C. is the easiest to nail   D. is the easiest to handle

14. A tool used in hanging doors is a   14.____

   A. miter gauge   B. line level
   C. try square   D. butt gauge

15. Of the following, the MAXIMUM height that would be considered acceptable for a stair   15.____
riser is

   A. 6 1/2"   B. 7 1/2"   C. 8 1/2"   D. 9 1/2"

16. The PRINCIPAL reason for *cross banding* the layers of wood in a plywood panel is to   16.____
_____ of the panel.

   A. reduce warping   B. increase the strength
   C. reduce the cost   D. increase the beauty

17. The part of a tree that will produce the DENSEST wood is the _____ wood.   17.____

   A. spring   B. summer   C. sap   D. heart

18. Casing nails MOST NEARLY resemble _____ nails.   18.____

   A. common   B. roofing   C. form   D. finishing

19. Lumber in quantity is ordered by   19.____

   A. cubic feet   B. foot board measure
   C. lineal feet   D. weight and length

20. For finishing of wood, BEST results are obtained by sanding   20.____

   A. with a circular motion
   B. against the grain
   C. with the grain
   D. with a circular motion on edges and against the grain on the flat parts

21. A *chase* in a brick wall is a   21.____

   A. pilaster   B. waterstop   C. recess   D. corbel

22. Parging refers to   22.____

   A. increasing the thickness of a brick wall
   B. plastering the back of face brickwork
   C. bonding face brick to backing blocks
   D. leveling each course of brick

23. The PRINCIPAL reason for requiring brick to be wetted before laying is that   23.____

    A. less water is required in the mortar
    B. efflorescence is prevented
    C. the brick will not absorb as much water from the mortar
    D. cool brick is easier to handle

24. In brickwork, muriatic acid is commonly used to   24.____

    A. increase the strength of the mortar
    B. etch the brick
    C. waterproof the wall
    D. clean the wall

25. Cement mortar can be made easier to work by the addition of a small quantity of   25.____

    A. lime   B. soda   C. litharge   D. plaster

26. Headers in brickwork are used to _____ the wall.   26.____

    A. strengthen   B. reduce the cost of
    C. speed the erection of   D. align

27. Joints in brick walls are tooled   27.____

    A. immediately after each brick is laid
    B. after the mortar has had its initial set
    C. after the entire wall is completed
    D. 28 days after the wall has been built

28. If cement mortar has begun to set before it can be used in a wall, the BEST thing to do is to   28.____

    A. use the mortar immediately as is
    B. add a small quantity of lime
    C. add some water and mix thoroughly
    D. discard the mortar

29. A *bat* in brickwork is a   29.____

    A. brace to hold a wall temporarily in place
    B. stick used to aid in mixing of mortar
    C. broken piece of brick used to fill short spaces
    D. curved brick used in ornamental work

30. The proportions by volume of cement, lime, and sand in a cement-lime mortar should be, according to the Building Code,   30.____

    A. 1:1:3   B. 2:1:6   C. 1:1:6   D. 1:2:6

31. The BEST flux to use when soldering galvanized iron is   31.____

    A. killed acid   B. sal-ammoniac
    C. muriatic acid   D. resin

32. When soldering a vertical joint, the soldering iron should be tinned on _____ side(s).   32.____

    A. 1   B. 2   C. 3   D. 4

33. The difference between *right hand* and *left hand* tin snips is the   33.____

    A. relative position of the cutting jaws
    B. shape of the cutting jaws
    C. shape of the handles
    D. relative position of the handles

34. A machine used to bend sheet metal is called a   34.____

    A. router   B. planer   C. brake   D. swage

35. The type of solder that would be used in *hard soldering* would be _____ solder.   35.____

    A. bismuth   B. wiping   C. 50-50   D. silver

36. Roll roofing material is usually felt which has been impregnated with   36.____

    A. cement   B. mastic   C. tar   D. latex

37. The purpose of flashing on roofs is to   37.____

    A. secure roofing materials to the roof
    B. make it easier to lay the roofing
    C. prevent leaks through the roof
    D. insulate the roof from excessive heat

38. The tool used to spread hot pitch on a three-ply roofing job is a   38.____

    A. mop   B. spreader   C. pusher   D. broom

39. The cutting of glass can be facilitated by dipping the cutting wheel in   39.____

    A. *3-in-1* oil   B. water   C. lard   D. kerosene

40. The strips of metal used to hold glass to the window frame while it is being puttied are called   40.____

    A. hold-downs   B. points   C. wedges   D. triangles

41. The type of chain used with sash weights is _____ link.   41.____

    A. flat   B. round
    C. figure-eight   D. basket-weave

42. The material that would be used to seal around a window frame is   42.____

    A. oakum   B. litharge   C. grout   D. calking

43. The function of a window sill is MOST NEARLY the same as that of a   43.____

    A. jamb   B. coping   C. lintel   D. brick

44. Lightweight plaster would be made with   44.____

    A. sand   B. cinders   C. potash   D. vermiculite

45. The FIRST coat of plaster to be applied on a three-coat plaster job is the _____ coat.   45.____

    A. brown   B. scratch   C. white   D. keene

46. Screeds in plaster work are used to   46.____

    A. remove larger sizes of sand
    B. hold the batch of plaster before it is applied
    C. apply the plaster to the wall
    D. guide the plasterer in making, an even wall

47. The FIRST coat of plaster over rock lath should be a _____ plaster.   47.____

    A. gypsum   B. lime
    C. portland cement   D. puzzolan cement

48. In plastering, a *hawk* is used to _____ plaster.   48.____

    A. apply   B. hold   C. scratch   D. smooth

49. When mixing concrete by hand, the order in which the ingredients should be mixed is: 49.____

    A. water, cement, sand, stone
    B. sand, cement, water, stone
    C. stone, water, sand, cement
    D. stone, sand, cement, water

50. The PRINCIPAL reason for covering a concrete sidewalk with straw or paper after the   50.____
    concrete has been poured is to

    A. prevent people from walking on the concrete while it is still wet
    B. impart a rough non-slip surface to the concrete
    C. prevent excessive evaporation of water in the concrete
    D. shorten the length of time it would take for the concrete to harden

---

KEY (CORRECT ANSWERS)

1. B	11. D	21. C	31. C	41. A
2. B	12. B	22. B	32. A	42. D
3. C	13. B	23. C	33. A	43. B
4. C	14. D	24. D	34. C	44. D
5. D	15. B	25. A	35. D	45. B
6. C	16. A	26. A	36. C	46. D
7. A	17. D	27. B	37. C	47. A
8. D	18. D	28. D	38. A	48. B
9. A	19. B	29. C	39. D	49. D
10. C	20. C	30. C	40. B	50. C

TEST 2

DIRECTIONS: Each question or incomplete statement is followed by several suggested answers or completions. Select the one that BEST answers the question or completes the statement. *PRINT THE LETTER OF THE CORRECT ANSWER IN THE SPACE AT THE RIGHT.*

1. When colored concrete is required, the colors used should be   1.____

    A.   colors in oil   B.   mineral pigments
    C.   tempera colors   D.   water colors

2. Concrete is *rubbed* with a(n)   2.____

    A.   emery wheel   B.   carborundum brick
    C.   sandstone   D.   alundum stick

3. To prevent concrete from sticking to forms, the forms should be painted with   3.____

    A.   oil   B.   kerosene   C.   water   D.   lime

4. The reinforcement in a concrete floor slab is referred to as 6"-6" x #6-#6.   4.____
The type of reinforcing that is being used is

    A.   steel bars   B.   wire mesh
    C.   angle irons   D.   grating plate

5. One method of measuring the consistency of a concrete mix is by means of a _____   5.____
test.

    A.   penetration   B.   flow   C.   slump   D.   weight

6. A chemical that is sometimes used to prevent the freezing of concrete in cold weather is 6.____

    A.   alum   B.   glycerine
    C.   calcium chloride   D.   sodium nitrate

7. The one of the following that is LEAST commonly used for columns is   7.____

    A.   wide flange beams   B.   angles
    C.   concrete-filled pipe   D.   *I* beams

8. Fire protection of steel floor beams is MOST frequently accomplished by the use of   8.____

    A.   gypsum block   B.   brick
    C.   rock wool fill   D.   vermiculite gypsum plaster

9. A *Pittsburgh lock* is a(n)   9.____

    A.   emergency door lock   B.   sheet metal joint
    C.   elevator safety   D.   boiler valve

10. In order to drill a hole at right angle to the horizontal axis of a round bar, the bar should   10.___
be held in a

    A.   step block   B.   C-block
    C.   hand pliers   D.   V-block

11. The procedure to follow in the lubrication of maintenance shop equipment is to lubricate   11.____

    A. when you can spare the time
    B. only when necessary
    C. at regular intervals
    D. when the equipment is in operation

12. Of the following items, the one which is NOT used in making fastenings to masonry or plaster walls is a(n)   12.____

    A. lead shield   B. expansion bolt
    C. rawl plug   D. steel bushing

13. When a common straight ladder is used to paint a wall, the safe distance that the foot of the ladder should be set away from the wall is MOST NEARLY _____ the length of the ladder.   13.____

    A. one-eighth   B. one-quarter
    C. one-half   D. five-eighths

14. The term *bell and spigot* usually refers to   14.____

    A. refrigerator motors   B. cast iron pipes
    C. steam radiator outlets   D. electrical receptacles

15. In plumbing work, a valve which allows water to flow in one direction only is commonly known as a _____ valve.   15.____

    A. check   B. globe   C. gate   D. stop

16. A pipe coupling is BEST used to connect two pieces of pipe of   16.____

    A. the same diameter in a straight line
    B. the same diameter at right angles to each other
    C. different diameters at a 45° angle
    D. different diameters at an 1/8th bend

17. A fitting or pipe with many outlets relatively close together is commonly called a   17.____

    A. manifold   B. gooseneck
    C. flange union   D. return bend

18. To locate the center in the end of a sound shaft, the BEST tool to use is a(n)   18.____

    A. ruler   B. divider
    C. hermaphrodite caliper   D. micrometer

19. When cutting a piece of 1 1/4" O.D. 20 gauge brass tubing with a hand hacksaw, it is BEST to use a blade having _____ teeth per inch.   19.____

    A. 14   B. 18   C. 22   D. 32

20. When cutting a piece of 1" O.D. extra-heavy pipe with a pipe cutter, a burr usually forms on the inside and the outside of the pipe. These burrs are BEST removed by means of a pipe   20.____

    A. tap and a file   B. wrench and rough stone
    C. reamer and a file   D. drill and a chisel

21. Artificial respiration should be started immediately on a man who has suffered an electric shock if he is

    A. *unconscious* and breathing
    B. *unconscious* and not breathing
    C. *conscious* and in a daze
    D. *conscious* and badly burned

21.____

22. The fuse of a certain circuit has blown and is replaced with a fuse of the same rating which also blows when the switch is closed.
    In this case,

    A. a fuse of higher current rating should be used
    B. a fuse of higher voltage rating should be used
    C. the fuse should be temporarily replaced by a heavy piece of wire
    D. the circuit should be checked

22.____

23. Operating an incandescent electric light bulb at less than its rated voltage will result in

    A. shorter life and brighter light
    B. longer life and dimmer light
    C. brighter light and longer life
    D. dimmer light and shorter life

23.____

24. In order to control a lamp from two different positions, it is necessary to use

    A. two single pole switches
    B. one single pole switch and one four-way switch
    C. two three-way switches
    D. one single pole switch and one four-way switch

24.____

25.

One method of testing fuses is to connect a pair of test lamps in the circuit in such a manner that the test lamp will light up if the fuse is good and will remain dark if the fuse is bad. In the above illustration 1 and 2 are fuses.
In order to test if fuse 1 is bad, test lamps should be connected between

    A. A and B   B. B and D   C. A and D   D. C and B

25.____

26. The PRINCIPAL reason for the grounding of electrical equipment and circuits is to

    A. prevent short circuits   B. insure safety from shock
    C. save power   D. increase voltage

26.____

27. The ordinary single-pole flush wall type switch must be connected   27.____

    A. across the line   B. in the *hot* conductor
    C. in the grounded conductor   D. in the white conductor

28. A D.C. shunt motor runs in the wrong direction. This fault can be CORRECTED by   28.____

    A. reversing the connections of both the field and the armature
    B. interchanging the connections of either main or auxiliar windings
    C. interchanging the connections to either the field or the armature windings
    D. interchanging the connections to the line of the power leads

29. The MOST common type of motor that can be used with both A.C. and D.C. sources is   29.____
the _____ motor.

    A. compound   B. repulsion   C. series   D. shunt

30. A fluorescent fixture in a new building has been in use for several months without trouble.   30.____
Recently, the ends of the fluorscent lamp have remained lighted when the light was
switched off.
The BEST way to clear up this trouble is to replace the

    A. lamp   B. ballast   C. starter   D. sockets

31. The BEST wood to use for handles of tools such as axes and hammers is   31.____

    A. hemlock   B. pine   C. oak   D. hickory

32. A *hanger bolt*   32.____

    A. has a square head
    B. is bent in a *U* shape
    C. has a different type of thread at each end
    D. is threaded the entire length from point to head

33. A stone frequently used to sharpen tools is   33.____

    A. carborundum   B. bauxite   C. resin   D. slate

34. A strike plate is MOST closely associated with a   34.____

    A. lock   B. sash   C. butt   D. tie rod

35. The material that distinguishes a terrazzo floor from an ordinary concrete floor is   35.____

    A. cinders   B. marble chip
    C. cut stone   D. non-slip aggregate

36. A room is 7'6" wide by 9'0" long with a ceiling height of 8'0". One gallon of flat paint will   36.____
cover approximately 400 square feet of wall.
The number of gallons of this paint required to paint the walls of this room, making no
deductions for windows or doors, is MOST NEARLY _____ gallon.

    A. 1/4   B. 1/2   C. 3/4   D. 1

37. The cost of a certain job is broken down as follows:

    Materials $375
    Rental of equipment   120
    Labor   315

    The percentage of the total cost of the job that can be charged to materials is MOST NEARLY

    A. 40%   B. 42%   C. 44%   D. 46%   37.___

38. By trial, it is found that by using two cubic feet of sand, a five cubic foot batch of concrete is produced.
    Using the same proportions, the amount of sand required to produce 2 cubic yards of concrete is MOST NEARLY _____ cu.ft.

    A. 20   B. 22   C. 24   D. 26   38.___

39. It takes 4 men 6 days to do a certain job.
    Working at the same speed, the number of days it will take 3 men to do this job is

    A. 7   B. 8   C. 9   D. 10   39.___

40. The cost of rawl plugs is $2.75 per gross. The cost of 2,448 rawl plugs is

    A. $46.75   B. $47.25   C. $47.75   D. $48.25   40.___

41. *Rigidity of the hammer handle enables the operator to control and direct the force of the blow.*
    As used above, *rigidity* means MOST NEARLY   41.___

    A. straightness   B. strength
    C. shape   D. stiffness

42. *For precision work, center punches are ground to a fine tapered point.* As used above, *tapered* means MOST NEARLY   42.___

    A. conical   B. straight   C. accurate   D. smooth

43. *There are limitations to the drilling of metals by hand power.*
    As used above, *limitations* means MOST NEARLY   43.___

    A. advantages   B. restrictions
    C. difficulties   D. benefits

Questions 44-45.

DIRECTIONS: Questions 44 and 45 are based on the following paragraph.

Because electric drills run at high speed, the cutting edges of a twist drill are heated quickly. If the metal is thick, the drill point must be withdrawn from the hole frequently to cool it and clear out chips. Forcing the drill continuously into a deep hole will heat it, thereby spoiling its temper and cutting edges. A portable electric drill has the advantage that it can be taken to the work and used to drill holes in material too large to handle in a drill press.

44. According to the above paragraph, overheating of a twist drill will   44.___

    A. slow down the work   B. cause excessive drill breakage
    C. dull the drill   D. spoil the accuracy of the work

45. According to the above paragraph, one method of preventing overheating of a twist drill is 45.____
    to

    A. use cooling oil
    B. drill a smaller pilot hole first
    C. use a drill press
    D. remove the drill from the work frequently

Questions 46-50.

DIRECTIONS: Questions 46 to 50 are to be answered in accordance with the sketch shown below.

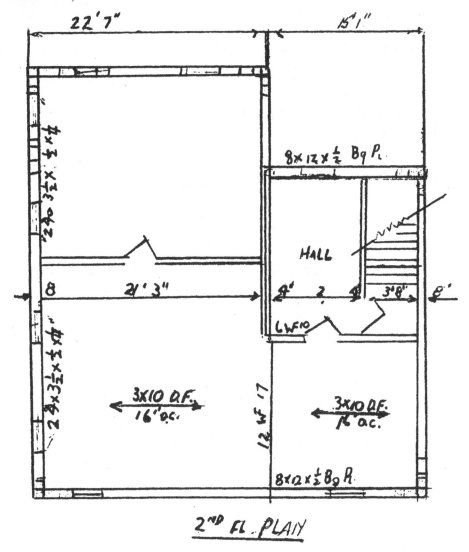

46. The one of the following statements that is CORRECT is the building 46.____

    A. is of fireproof construction
    B. has masonry walls with wood joists
    C. is of wood frame construction
    D. has timber joists and girders

47. The one of the following statements that is CORRECT is 47.___
    A. the stairway from the ground continues through the roof
    B. there are two means of egress from the second floor of this building
    C. the door on the second floor stair landing opens in the direction of egress
    D. the entire stair is shown on this plan

48. The width of the hall is 48.___
    A. 10'3"   B. 10'5"   C. 10'7"   D. 10'9"

49. The lintels shown are 49.___
    A. angles   B. a channel and an angle
    C. an I-beam   D. precast concrete

50. The one of the following statements that is CORRECT is that the steel beam is 50.___
    A. supported by columns at the center and at the ends
    B. entirely supported by the walls
    C. supported on columns at the ends only
    D. supported at the center by a column and at the ends by the walls

---

KEY (CORRECT ANSWERS)

1. B	11. C	21. B	31. D	41. D
2. B	12. D	22. D	32. C	42. A
3. A	13. B	23. B	33. A	43. B
4. B	14. B	24. C	34. A	44. C
5. C	15. A	25. C	35. B	45. D
6. C	16. A	26. B	36. C	46. B
7. B	17. A	27. B	37. D	47. C
8. D	18. C	28. C	38. B	48. D
9. B	19. D	29. C	39. B	49. A
10. D	20. C	30. C	40. A	50. D

EXAMINATION SECTION
TEST 1

DIRECTIONS: Each question or incomplete statement is followed by several suggested answers or completions. Select the one that BEST answers the question or completes the statement. *PRINT THE LETTER OF THE CORRECT ANSWER IN THE SPACE AT THE RIGHT.*

1. Linseed oil putty would MOST likely be used to secure glass in _____ windows.　　1._____

    A. steel casement 　　　　　　　　B. aluminum jalousie
    C. wood double hung 　　　　　　　D. aluminum storm

2. Of the following, the one type of glass that should NOT be cut with the ordinary type glass cutter is _____ glass.　　2._____

    A. safety 　　　　B. plate 　　　　C. wire 　　　　D. herculite

3. Thermopane is made of two sheets of glass separated by　　3._____

    A. a sheet of celluloid 　　　　　　B. wire mesh
    C. an air space 　　　　　　　　　D. mica

4. Glass is NEVER cut so that it fits snugly inside the frame of a steel casement window. Of the following, the MAIN reason for allowing this space between the glass and the side of the frame is to　　4._____

    A. prevent cracking of the glass in cold weather
    B. permit the glass to be lined up properly
    C. allow space for the putty
    D. eliminate the necessity of polishing the edges of the glass

5. Glass is held in steel sash by means of　　5._____

    A. points 　　　　B. clips 　　　　C. plates 　　　　D. blocks

6. When nailing felt to a roof, the nails should be driven through a　　6._____

    A. tinned disc 　　　　　　　　　B. steel washer
    C. brass plate 　　　　　　　　　D. plastic bushing

7. An opening in a parapet wall for draining water from a roof is MOST often called a　　7._____

    A. leader 　　　　B. gutter 　　　　C. downspout 　　　　D. scupper

8. Roofing nails are usually　　8._____

    A. brass 　　　　　　　　　　　B. cement coated
    C. galvanized 　　　　　　　　　D. nickel plated

9. A *street ell* is a fitting having　　9._____

    A. male threads at both ends
    B. male threads at one end and female threads at the other end
    C. female threads at both ends
    D. male threads at one end and a solder connection at the other end

10. Of the following pieces of equipment, the one on which you would MOST likely find a safety (pop-off) valve is a(n)   10.___

    A.   hot air furnace
    B.   air conditioning compressor
    C.   hot water heater
    D.   dehumidifier

11. Compression fittings are MOST often used with   11.___

    A.   cast iron bell and spigot pipe
    B.   steel flange pipe
    C.   copper tubing
    D.   transite

12. Water hammer is BEST eliminated by   12.___

    A.   increasing the size of all the piping
    B.   installing an air chamber
    C.   replacing the valve seats with neoprene gaskets
    D.   flushing the system to remove corrosion

13. The BEST type of pipe to use in a gas line in a domestic installation is   13.___

    A.   black iron   B.   galvanized iron
    C.   cast iron   D.   wrought steel

14. If there is a pinhole in the float of a toilet tank, the   14.___

    A.   water will flush continually
    B.   toilet cannot flush
    C.   tank cannot be filled with water
    D.   valve will not shut off so water will overflow into the overflow tube

15. Condensation of moisture in humid weather occurs MOST often on _____ pipe(s).   15.___

    A.   sewage   B.   gas
    C.   hot water   D.   cold water

16. A gas appliance should be connected to a gas line by means of a(n)   16.___

    A.   union   B.   right and left coupling
    C.   elbow   D.   close nipple

17. A PRINCIPAL difference between a pipe thread and a machine thread is that the pipe thread is   17.___

    A.   tapered   B.   finer   C.   flat   D.   longer

18. When joining galvanized iron pipe, pipe joint compound is placed on   18.___

    A.   the female threads only
    B.   the male threads only
    C.   both the male and female threads
    D.   either the male or the female threads depending on the type of fitting

19. If moisture is trapped between the layers of a 3-ply roof, the heat of a summer day will   19.____

    A. dry the roof out
    B. cause blisters to be formed in the roofing
    C. rot the felt material
    D. have no effect on the roofing

20. Of the following, the metal MOST often used for leaders and gutters is   20.____

    A. monel   B. brass
    C. steel   D. galvanized iron

21. When drilling a small hole in sheet copper, the BEST practice is to   21.____

    A. make a dent with a center punch first
    B. put some cutting oil at the point you intend to drill
    C. use a slow speed drill to prevent overheating
    D. use an auger type bit

22. The reason for annealing sheet copper is to make it   22.____

    A. soft and easier to work
    B. more resistant to weather
    C. easier to solder
    D. harder and more resistant to blows

23. In draw filing,   23.____

    A. only the edge of the file is used
    B. a triangle file is generally used
    C. the file is pulled toward the mechanic's body in filing
    D. the file must have a safe edge

24. The type of paint that uses water as a thinner is   24.____

    A. enamel   B. latex   C. shellac   D. lacquer

25. The reason for placing a 6" sub-base of cinders under a concrete sidewalk is to   25.____

    A. provide flexibility in the surface
    B. permit drainage of water
    C. prevent chemicals in the soil from damaging the sidewalk
    D. allow room for the concrete to expand

26. The BEST material to use to lubricate a door lock is   26.____

    A. penetrating oil   B. pike oil
    C. graphite   D. light grease

27. Assume that the color of the flame from a gas stove is bright yellow.
To correct this, you should   27.____

    A. close the air flap
    B. open the air flap
    C. increase the gas pressure
    D. increase the size of the gas opening

28. In a 110-220 volt three-wire circuit, the neutral wire is usually   28.__

    A. black   B. red   C. white   D. green

29. Brushes on fractional horsepower universal motors are MOST often made of   29.__

    A. flexible copper strands   B. rigid carbon blocks
    C. thin wire strips   D. collector rings

30. Leaks from the stem of a faucet can generally be stopped by replacing the   30.__

    A. bibb washer   B. seat   C. packing   D. gasket

31. Of the following, the BEST procedure to follow with a frozen water pipe is to   31.__

    A. allow the pipe to thaw out by itself as the weather gets warmer
    B. put anti-freeze into the pipe above the section that is frozen
    C. turn on the hot water heater
    D. open the faucet closest to the frozen pipe and warm the pipe with a blow torch, starting at this point

32. The one of the following that is NOT usually changed by a central air conditioning system is the   32.__

    A. volume of air in the system   B. humidity of the air
    C. dust in the air   D. air pressure of the system

33. The temperature of a domestic hot water system is MOST often controlled by a(n)   33.__

    A. relief valve   B. aquastat   C. barometer   D. thermostat

34. Draft in a chimney is MOST often controlled by a(n)   34.__

    A. damper   B. gate
    C. orifice   D. cross connection

35. Assume that a refrigerator motor operates continuously for excessively long periods of time.   35.__
The FIRST item you should check to locate the defect is the

    A. plug in the outlet
    B. door gasket
    C. direction of rotation of the motor
    D. motor switch

36. Assume that after replacing a defective motor for a large electric fan, you find that the fan is rotating in the wrong direction.   36.__
If the motor is a split phase motor, with the shaft at one end only, the trouble could be CORRECTED by

    A. reversing the fan on its shaft
    B. turning the motor end for end
    C. interchanging the connections on the field terminals of the motor
    D. reversing the plug in the electric outlet

37. In order to properly hang a door, shims are frequently inserted under the hinges.   37.____
    These shims are MOST often made of

    A. cardboard
    B. sheet steel
    C. bakelite
    D. the same materials as the hinges

38. Flooring nails are usually _____ nails.   38.____

    A. casing   B. common   C. cut   D. clinch

39. Over a doorway, to support brick, you will usually find   39.____

    A. steel angles   B. hanger bolts
    C. wooden headers   D. stirrups

40. Insulation of steam pipes is MOST often done with   40.____

    A. asbestos   B. celotex   C. alundum   D. sheathing

41. Assume that only the first few coils of a hot water convector used for heating a room are   41.____
    hot.
    To correct this, you should FIRST

    A. increase the water pressure
    B. increase the water temperature
    C. bleed the air out of the convector
    D. clean the convector pipes

42. The MAIN reason for grounding the outer sheel of an electric fixture is to   42.____

    A. provide additional support for the fixture
    B. reduce the cost of installation of the fixture
    C. provide a terminal to which the wires can be attached
    D. reduce the chance of electric shock

43. In woodwork, countersinking is MOST often done for   43.____

    A. lag screws   B. carriage bolts
    C. hanger bolts   D. flat head screws

44. Bridging is MOST often used in connection with   44.____

    A. door frames   B. window openings
    C. floor joists   D. stud walls

45. A saddle is part of a   45.____

    A. doorway   B. window
    C. stair well   D. bulkhead

46. To make it easier to drive screws into hard wood, it is BEST to 46.___

    A. use a screwdriver that is longer than that used for soft wood
    B. rub the threads of the screw on a bar of soap
    C. oil the screw threads
    D. use a square shank screwdriver assisted by a wrench

47. In using a doweled joint to make a repair of a wooden door, it is important to remember that the dowel 47.___

    A. hole must be smaller in diameter than the dowel so that there is a tight fit
    B. hole must be longer than the dowel to provide a room for excess glue
    C. must be of the same type of wood as the door frame
    D. must be held in place by a small screw while waiting for the glue to set

48. The edges of MOST finished wood flooring are 48.___

    A. tongue and groove   B. mortise and tenon
    C. bevel and miter   D. lap and scarf

49. For the SMOOTHEST finish, sanding of wood should be done 49.___

    A. in a circular direction
    B. diagonally against the grain
    C. across the grain
    D. parallel with the grain

50. To prevent splintering of wood when boring a hole through it, the BEST practice is to 50.___

    A. drill at a slow speed
    B. use a scrap piece to back up the work
    C. use an auger bit
    D. ease up the pressure on the drill when the drill is almost through the wood

---

KEY (CORRECT ANSWERS)

1. C	11. C	21. A	31. D	41. C
2. D	12. B	22. A	32. D	42. D
3. C	13. A	23. C	33. B	43. D
4. A	14. D	24. B	34. A	44. C
5. B	15. D	25. B	35. B	45. A
6. A	16. B	26. C	36. C	46. B
7. D	17. A	27. B	37. A	47. B
8. C	18. B	28. C	38. C	48. A
9. B	19. B	29. B	39. A	49. D
10. C	20. D	30. C	40. A	50. B

TEST 2

DIRECTIONS: Each question or incomplete statement is followed by several suggested answers or completions. Select the one that BEST answers the question or completes the statement. *PRINT THE LETTER OF THE CORRECT ANSWER IN THE SPACE AT THE RIGHT.*

1. A *speed nut* has

   A. no threads
   B. threads that are coarser than a standard nut
   C. threads that are finer than s standard nut
   D. fewer threads than a standard nut

1.____

2. The BEST tool to use to remove the burr and sharp edge resulting from cutting tubing with a tube cutter is a

   A. file   B. scraper   C. reamer   D. knife

2.____

3. A router is used PRINCIPALLY to

   A. clean pipe   B. cut grooves in wood
   C. bend electric conduit   D. sharpen tools

3.____

4. The principle of operation of a sabre saw is MOST similar to that of a _____ saw.

   A. circular   B. radial   C. swing   D. jig

4.____

5. A full thread cutting set would have both taps and

   A. cutters   B. bushings   C. dies   D. plugs

5.____

6. The proper flux to use for soldering electric wire connections is

   A. rosin   B. killed acid
   C. borax   D. zinc chloride

6.____

7. A fusestat differs from an ordinary plug fuse in that a fusestat has

   A. less current carrying capacity
   B. different size threads
   C. an aluminum shell instead of a copper shell
   D. no threads

7.____

8. A grounding type 120-volt receptacle differs from an ordinary electric receptacle MAINLY in that a grounding receptacle

   A. is larger than the ordinary receptacle
   B. has openings for a three prong plug
   C. can be used for larger machinery
   D. has a built-in circuit breaker

8.____

9. A carbide tip is MOST often found on a bit used for drilling

   A. concrete   B. wood   C. steel   D. brass

9.____

10. The MAIN reason for using oil on an oilstone is to

    A. make the surface of the stone smoother
    B. prevent clogging of the pores of the stone
    C. reduce the number of times the stone has to be *dressed*
    D. prevent gouging of the stone's surface

10.____

11. The sum of the following numbers, 1 3/4, 3 1/6, 5 1/2, 6 5/8, and 9 1/4, is

    A. 26 1/8   B. 26 1/4   C. 26 1/2   D. 26 3/4

11.____

12. If a piece of plywood measures 5' 1 1/4" x 3' 2 1/2", the number of square feet in this board is MOST NEARLY

    A. 15.8   B. 16.1   C. 16.4   D. 16.7

12.____

13. Assume that in quantity purchases the city receives a discount of 33 1/3%.
If a one gallon can of paint retails at $5.33 per gallon, the cost of 375 gallons of this paint is MOST NEARLY

    A. $1,332.50   B. $1,332.75   C. $1,333.00   D. $1,333.25

13.____

14. Assume that eight barrels of cement together weigh a total of 3004 lbs. and 12 oz.
If there are four bags of cement per barrel, then the weight of one bag of cement is MOST NEARLY _____ lbs.

    A. 93.1   B. 93.5   C. 93.9   D. 94.3

14.____

15. Assume that one man cuts 50 nameplates per hour, whereas his co-worker cuts 55 nameplates per hour.
At the end of 7 hours, the first man will have cut fewer nameplates than the second man by

    A. 9.3%   B. 9.5%   C. 9.7%   D. 9.9%

15.____

16. Under the same conditions, the one of the following that dries the FASTEST is

    A. shellac   B. varnish   C. enamel   D. lacquer

16.____

17. Interior wood trim in a building is MOST often made of

    A. hemlock   B. pine   C. cedar   D. oak

17.____

18. Gaskets are seldom made of

    A. rubber   B. lead   C. asbestos   D. vinyl

18.____

19. Toggle bolts are MOST frequently used to

    A. fasten shelf supports to a hollow block wall
    B. fasten furniture legs to table tops
    C. anchor machinery to a concrete floor
    D. join two pieces of sheet metal

19.____

20. Rubber will deteriorate FASTEST when it is constantly in contact with

    A. air   B. water   C. oil   D. soapsuds

20.____

21. Stoppage of water flow is often caused by dirt <u>accumulating</u> in an elbow.
As used in the above sentence, the word <u>accumulating</u> means MOST NEARLY

    A. clogging   B. collecting   C. rusting   D. confined

21.____

22. The surface of the metal was <u>embossed</u>.
As used in the above sentence, the word <u>embossed</u> means MOST NEARLY

    A. polished   B. rough   C. raised   D. painted

22.____

Questions 23-24.

DIRECTIONS: Questions 23 and 24 are to be answered in accordance with the following paragraph.

When fixing an upper sash cord, you must also remove the lower sash. To do this, the parting strip between the sash must be removed. Now remove the cover from the weight box channel, cut off the cord as before, and pull it over the pulleys. Pull your new cord over the pulleys and down into the channel, where it may be fastened to the weight. The cord for an upper sash is cut off 1" or 2" below the pulley with the weight resting on the floor of the pocket and the cord held taut. These measurements allow for slight stretching of the cord. When the cord is cut to length, it can be pulled up over the pulley and tied with a single common knot in the end to fit into the socket in the sash groove. If the knot protrudes beyond the face of the sash, tap it gently to flatten. In this way, it will not become frayed from constant rubbing against the groove.

23. When repairing the upper sash cord, the FIRST thing to do is to

    A. remove the lower sash
    B. cut the existing sash cord
    C. remove the parting strip
    D. measure the length of new cord necessary

23.____

24. According to the above paragraph, the rope may become frayed if the

    A. pulley is too small   B. knot sticks out
    C. cord is too long   D. weight is too heavy

24.____

25. In the repair of the sash cord mentioned in the paragraph for Questions 23 and 24, the MAIN reason for cutting off the sash cord below the bottom of the pulley is to

    A. prevent the cord from tangling
    B. save on amount of cord used
    C. prevent the sash weight from hitting the bottom of the frame in use
    D. provide room for tying the knot

25.____

26. Of the following drawings, the one that would be considered an *elevation* of a building is the

    A. floor plan   B. front view   C. cross section   D. site plan

26.____

27. On a plan, the symbol shown at the right USUALLY represents a(n)

    A. duplex receptacle   B. electric switch
    C. ceiling outlet   D. pull box

27.____

28. On a plan, the symbol _____ - _____ - USUALLY represents a
    A. center line B. hidden outline
    C. long break D. dimension line

28._____

29. Assume that on a plan you see the following: 1/4" - 20 NC-2. This refers to the

29._____
    A. diameter of a hole
    B. size and type of screw thread
    C. taper of a pin
    D. scale at which the plan is drawn

30.

30._____

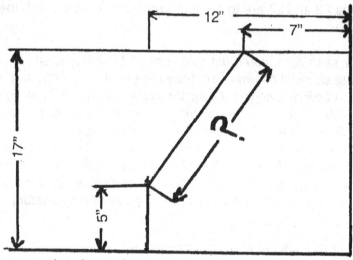

In reference to the above sketch, the length of the diagonal part of the plate indicated by the question mark is MOST NEARLY

    A. 13"   B. 14"   C. 15"   D. 16"

31. To increase the workability of concrete without changing its strength, the BEST procedure to follow is to increase the percentage of

31._____
    A. water   B. cement and sand
    C. cement and water   D. water and sand

32. The MAIN reason for covering freshly poured concrete with tar paper is to

32._____
    A. prevent evaporation of water
    B. stop people from walking on the concrete
    C. protect the concrete from rain
    D. keep back any earth that may fall on the concrete

33. The MAIN reason for using air-entrained cement in sidewalks is to

33._____
    A. protect the concrete from the effects of freezing
    B. color the concrete
    C. speed up the setting time of the concrete
    D. make the concrete more workable

34. Assume that a reinforcing bar used for concrete is badly rusted. 34.____
Before using this bar,

    A. it is not necessary to remove any rust
    B. only loose rust need be removed
    C. all rust should be removed
    D. all rust should be removed and a coat of red lead paint is applied

35. Assume that freshly poured concrete has been exposed to freezing temperatures for 6 35.____
hours.
In all likelihood, this concrete

    A. has been permanently damaged
    B. will harden properly as soon as the air temperature warms up
    C. will harden properly even though the temperature remains below freezing
    D. will eventually harden properly, but it will take much longer than usual

36. Assume that concrete for a floor in a play yard is to be placed directly on the earth. On 36.____
checking, you find that, because of a recent rain, the earth is damp.
You should

    A. wait till the sun dries the earth before placing the concrete
    B. use a waterproofing material between the concrete slab and the earth
    C. use less water in the concrete mix
    D. ignore the damp earth and place the concrete as you normally would

37. The MAJOR disadvantage of *floating* the surface of concrete too much is that the 37.____

    A. surface will become too rough
    B. surface will become weak and will wear rapidly
    C. initial set will be disturbed
    D. concrete cannot be cured properly

38. In addition to water and sand, mortar mix for a cinder block wall is usually made of 38.____

    A. gravel and lime   B. plaster and cement
    C. gravel and cement   D. lime and cement

39. The *nominal* size of a standard cinder block is 39.____

    A. 8" x 6" x 16"   B. 8" x 8" x 16"
    C. 8" x 12" x 12"   D. 6" x 8" x 12"

40. The *bond* of a brick wall refers to the 40.____

    A. arrangement of headers and stretchers
    B. time it takes for the mortar to set
    C. way a brick wall is tied in to an intersecting wall
    D. type of mortar used in the wall

41. The purpose of *tooling* when erecting a brick wall is to 41.____

    A. cut the brick to fit into a small space
    B. insure that the brick is laid level
    C. compact the mortar at the joints
    D. hold the brick in place till the mortar sets

42. Mortar is BEST cleaned off the face of a brick wall by using   42.___

    A. muriatic acid   B. lye
    C. oxalic acid   D. sodium hypochlorite

43. A brick wall is *pointed* to   43.___

    A. make sure it is the correct height
    B. repair the mortar joints
    C. set the brick in place
    D. arrange the mortar bed before setting the brick

44. The second coat in a three-coat plaster job is the _____ coat.   44.___

    A. scratch   B. brown   C. putty   D. lime

45. To repair fine cracks in a plastered wall, the PROPER material to use is   45.___

    A. lime   B. cement wash
    C. perlite   D. spackle

46. Gypsum lath for plastering is purchased in   46.___

    A. strips 5/16" x 1 1/2" x 4'
    B. rolls 3/8" x 48" x 96"
    C. boards 1/2" x 16" x 48"
    D. sheets 5/16" x 27" x 96"

47. The PRINCIPAL reason for using acoustic tile instead of ordinary tile is that the acoustic   47.___
tile

    A. deadens sound   B. is easier to apply
    C. is longer lasting   D. costs less

48. The MAXIMUM thickness of the finish coat of white plaster is MOST NEARLY   48.___

    A. 1/8"   B. 1/4"   C. 3/8"   D. 1/2"

49. When using tape to conceal joints in dry wall construction, the FIRST operation is   49.___

    A. channelling the grooves between boards
    B. applying cement to the joints
    C. sanding the edges of the joints
    D. packing the tape into the joints

50. For the FIRST coat of plaster on wire lath, plaster of paris is mixed with   50.___

    A. cement   B. sand   C. lime   D. mortar

———

KEY (CORRECT ANSWERS)

1.	A	11.	B	21.	B	31.	C	41.	C
2.	C	12.	C	22.	C	32.	A	42.	A
3.	B	13.	A	23.	C	33.	A	43.	B
4.	D	14.	C	24.	B	34.	B	44.	B
5.	C	15.	D	25.	C	35.	A	45.	D
6.	A	16.	D	26.	B	36.	D	46.	C
7.	B	17.	B	27.	C	37.	B	47.	A
8.	B	18.	D	28.	A	38.	D	48.	A
9.	A	19.	A	29.	B	39.	B	49.	B
10.	B	20.	C	30.	A	40.	A	50.	B

EXAMINATION SECTION
TEST 1

DIRECTIONS: Each question or incomplete statement is followed by several suggested answers or completions. Select the one that BEST answers the question or completes the statement. *PRINT THE LETTER OF THE CORRECT ANSWER IN THE SPACE AT THE RIGHT.*

1. A bit is held in a hand drill by means of a(n)   1.____

    A. arbor   B. chuck   C. collet   D. clamp

2. The type of screw that MOST often requires a countersunk hole is a _____ head.   2.____

    A. flat   B. round   C. fillister   D. hexagon

3. Instead of using the ordinary 1 piece screwdriver, a screwdriver bit is MOST often used   3.____
with a brace because of the

    A. increased length of the brace   B. different types of bits available
    C. increased leverage of the brace   D. ability to work in tight corners

4. A thread gage is usually used to measure the   4.____

    A. thickness of a thread   B. diameter of a thread
    C. number of threads per inch   D. height of a thread

5. The wheel of a glass cutter is BEST lubricated with   5.____

    A. kerosene   B. linseed oil
    C. varnolene   D. diesel oil

6. A nail set is a   6.____

    A. group of nails of the same size and type
    B. group of nails of different sizes but the same type
    C. tool used to extract nails
    D. tool used to drive nails below the surface of wood

7. To test for leaks in a gas line, it is BEST to use   7.____

    A. a match   B. soapy water
    C. a colored dye   D. ammonia

8. Routing is the process of cutting a   8.____

    A. strip out of sheet metal   B. groove in wood
    C. chamfer on a shaft   D. core out of concrete

9. A hacksaw frame has a wing nut mainly to   9.____

    A. make it easier to replace blades
    B. increase the strength of the frame
    C. prevent vibration of the blade
    D. adjust the length of the frame

10. A mitre box is usually used with a _____ saw.　　　　　　　　　　　　　10.____

    A. hack　　　　　B. crosscut　　　　C. rip　　　　　D. back

11. A continuous flexible saw blade is MOST often used on a _____ saw.　　11.____

    A. radial　　　　B. band　　　　　C. swing　　　　D. table

12. A pipe reamer is used to　　　　　　　　　　　　　　　　　　　　　　12.____

    A. clean out a length of pipe
    B. thread pipe
    C. remove burrs from the ends of pipe
    D. seal pipe joints

13. To lay out a straight cut on a piece of wood at the same angle as the cut on a second　13.____
    piece of wood, the PROPER tool to use is a

    A. bevel　　　　B. cope　　　　　C. butt gauge　　D. clevis

14. Before drilling a hole in a piece of metal, an indentation should be made with a _____　14.____
    punch.

    A. pin　　　　　B. taper　　　　C. center　　　　D. drift

15. Curved cuts in wood are BEST made with a _____ saw.　　　　　　　　15.____

    A. jig　　　　　B. veneer　　　　C. radial　　　　D. swing

16. A face plate is generally used to　　　　　　　　　　　　　　　　　　16.____

    A. hold material while working with it on a lathe
    B. smooth out irregularities in a metal plate
    C. protect the finish on a metal plate
    D. locate centers of holes to be drilled on a drill press

17. A die would be used to　　　　　　　　　　　　　　　　　　　　　　17.____

    A. gage the groove in a splined shaft
    B. cut a thread on a metal rod
    C. hold a piece to be machined on a milling machine
    D. control the depth of a hole to be drilled in a piece of metal

18. Before using a ladle to scoop up molten solder, you should make sure that the ladle is　18.____
    dry.
    This is done to prevent

    A. the solder from sticking to the ladle
    B. impurities from getting into the solder
    C. injuries due to splashing solder
    D. cooling of the solder

19. To PROPERLY adjust the gap on a spark plug, you should use a(n)   19.____

    A. inside caliper   B. center gauge
    C. wire type feeler gauge   D. micrometer

20. The length of the MOST common type of folding wood rule is _____ feet.   20.____

    A. 4   B. 5   C. 6   D. 7

21. A four-foot mason's level is usually used to determine whether the top of a wall is level   21.____
    and whether it is

    A. square   B. plumb   C. rigid   D. in line

22. To match a tongue in a board, the matching board MUST have a   22.____

    A. rabbet   B. chamfer   C. bead   D. groove

23. When driving screws in close quarters, the BEST type of screwdriver to use is a(n)   23.____

    A. Phillips   B. offset   C. butt   D. angled

24. The term 12-24 refers to a _____ screw.   24.____

    A. wood   B. lag
    C. sheet metal   D. machine

25. To measure the length of a curved line on a drawing or plan, the PROPER tool to use in   25.____
    addition to a ruler is(are)

    A. dividers   B. calipers
    C. surface gage   D. radius gage

26. For the standard machine screw, the diameter of a tap drill is generally   26.____

    A. *equal* to the diameter of the shaft of the screw at the base of the threads (the root
        diameter)
    B. *larger* than the root diameter, but smaller than the diameter of the screw
    C. *equal* to the diameter of the screw
    D. *larger* than the diameter of the screw

27. In order to drill a 1" hole accurately with a drill press, you should   27.____

    A. drill at high speeds
    B. use very little pressure on the drill
    C. drill partway down, release pressure on the drill, and then continue drilling
    D. drill a pilot hole first

28. Before taking apart an electric motor to repair, punch marks are sometimes placed on   28.____
    the casing near each other.
    The MOST probable reason for doing this is to

    A. make sure the parts lock together on reassembly
    B. properly line up the parts that are next to each other
    C. keep track of the number of parts in the assembly
    D. identify all the parts as coming from the one motor

29. To locate a point on a floor directly under a point on the ceiling, the PROPER tool to use is a   29.____

    A. square   B. line level
    C. height gage   D. plumb bob

Question 30.

DIRECTIONS: Question 30 is based on the diagram appearing below.

P

200 lb

30. In the above diagram, the full P required to lift the weight a distance of four feet is MOST NEARLY _____ lbs.   30.____

    A. 50   B. 67   C. 75   D. 100

31. The EASIEST tool to use to determine whether the edge of a board is at right angles to the face of the board is a   31.____

    A. rafter square   B. try square
    C. protractor   D. marking gage

32. *Whetting* refers to   32.____

    A. tempering of tools by dipping them in water
    B. annealing of tools by heating and slow cooling
    C. brazing of carbide tips on tools
    D. sharpening of tools

33. The MOST difficult part of a plank to plane is the   33.____

    A. face   B. side   C. end   D. back

34. To prevent wood from splitting when drilling with an auger, it is BEST to   34.____

    A. use even pressure on the bit
    B. drill at a slow speed
    C. hold the wood tightly in a vise
    D. back up the wood with a piece of scrap wood

35. The term *dressing a grinding wheel* refers to   35.____

    A. setting up the wheel on the arbor
    B. restoring the sharpness of a wheel face that has become clogged
    C. placing flanges against the sides of the wheel
    D. bringing the wheel up to speed before using it

36. Heads of rivets are BEST cut off with a   36.____

    A. hacksaw   B. cold chisel
    C. fly cutter   D. reamer

37. A *V-block* is especially useful to   37.____

    A. prevent damage to work held in a vise
    B. hold round stock while a hole is being drilled into it
    C. prevent rolling of round stock stored on the ground
    D. shim up the end of a machine so that it is level

38. A full set of taps for a given size usually consists of a _____ tap.   38.____

    A. taper and bottoming
    B. taper and plug
    C. plug and bottoming
    D. taper, plug, and bottoming

39. Round thread cutting dies are usually held in stock by means of   39.____

    A. wing nuts   B. clamps   C. set screws   D. bolts

40. The one of the following diagrams that shows the plan view and the elevation of a counterbored hole is   40.____

A.

B.

C.

D.

41. With regard to pipe, *I.D.* usually means   41.____

    A. inside diameter   B. inside dressed
    C. invert diameter   D. installation date

42. A compression fitting is MOST often used to   42.____

    A. lubricate a wheel
    B. join two pieces of tubing
    C. reduce the diameter of a hole
    D. press fit a gear to a shaft

43. The shape of a mill file is basically   43.____

    A. flat   B. half round   C. triangular   D. square

44. Of the following, the ratio of tin to lead that will produce the solder with the LOWEST   44.____
melting point is

    A. 30-70   B. 40-60   C. 50-50   D. 60-40

45. A safe edge on a file is one that   45.____

    A. is smooth and can not cut
    B. has a finer cut than the face of the file
    C. is rounded to prevent scratches
    D. has a coarser cut than the face of the file

46. The MOST frequent use of a file card is to _____ files.   46.____

    A. sort out   B. clean
    C. prevent damage to   D. prevent clogging of

47. The BEST way of determining whether a grinding wheel has an internal crack is to   47.____

    A. run the wheel at high speed, stop it, and examine the wheel
    B. spray lubricating oil on the sides of the wheel and check the amount of absorption
       of the oil
    C. hit the wheel with a rubber hammer and listen to the sound
    D. drop the wheel sharply on a table and then check the wheel

48. If a grinding wheel has worn to a smaller diameter, the BEST practice to follow is to   48.____

    A. discard the wheel
    B. continue using the wheel as before
    C. use the wheel, but at a faster speed
    D. use the wheel, but at a slower speed

49. With respect to the ordinary awl,   49.____

    A. only the tip is hardened
    B. the entire blade is hardened
    C. the tip is tempered, and the rest of the blade is hardened
    D. the entire blade is tempered

50. To prevent overheating of drills, it is BEST to use _____ oil.   50.____

    A. cutting   B. lubricating
    C. penetrating   D. heating

KEY (CORRECT ANSWERS)

1.	B	11.	B	21.	B	31.	B	41.	A
2.	A	12.	C	22.	D	32.	D	42.	B
3.	C	13.	A	23.	B	33.	C	43.	A
4.	C	14.	C	24.	D	34.	D	44.	D
5.	A	15.	A	25.	A	35.	B	45.	A
6.	D	16.	A	26.	B	36.	B	46.	B
7.	B	17.	B	27.	D	37.	B	47.	C
8.	B	18.	C	28.	B	38.	D	48.	C
9.	A	19.	C	29.	D	39.	C	49.	A
10.	D	20.	C	30.	D	40.	A	50.	A

TEST 2

DIRECTIONS: Each question or incomplete statement is followed by several suggested answers or completions. Select the one that BEST answers the question or completes the statement. *PRINT THE LETTER OF THE CORRECT ANSWER IN THE SPACE AT THE RIGHT.*

1. Crocus cloth is commonly used to   1._____

    A. protect finely machined surfaces from damage while the machines are being repaired
    B. remove rust from steel
    C. protect floors and furniture while painting walls
    D. wipe up oil and grease that has spilled

2. Before using a new paint brush, the FIRST operation should be to   2._____

    A. remove loose bristles
    B. soak the brush in linseed oil
    C. hang the brush up overnight
    D. clean the brush with turpentine

3. When sharpening a hand saw, the FIRST operation is to   3._____

    A. file the teeth down to the same height
    B. shape the teeth to the proper profile
    C. bend the teeth over to provide clearance when sawing
    D. clean the gullies with a file

4. To prevent solder from dripping when soldering a vertical seam, it is BEST to   4._____

    A. hold a waxed rag under the soldering iron
    B. use the soldering iron in a horizontal position
    C. tin the soldering iron on one side only
    D. solder the seam in the order from bottom to top

5. If a round nut has two holes in the face, the PROPER type wrench to use to tighten this nut is a(n)   5._____

    A. Stillson   B. monkey   C. spanner   D. open end

6. A box wrench is BEST used on   6._____

    A. pipe fittings   B. flare nuts
    C. hexagonal nuts   D. Allen screws

7. To prevent damage to fine finishes on metal work that is to be held in a vise, you should   7._____

    A. clamp the work lightly
    B. use brass inserts on the vise
    C. wrap the work with cloth before inserting it in the vise
    D. substitute a smooth face plate for the serrated plate on the vise

8. The MOST frequent use for a turnbuckle is to   8.____

     A. tighten a guy wire
     B. adjust shims on a machine
     C. bolt a bracket to a wall
     D. support electric cable from a ceiling

9. To form the head of a tinner's rivet, the PROPER tool to use is a rivet   9.____

     A. anvil   B. plate   C. set   D. brake

10. A socket speed handle MOST closely resembles a   10.____

     A. screwdriver   B. brace   C. spanner   D. spin grip

11. Tips of masonry drills are usually made of   11.____

     A. steel   B. carbide   C. corundum   D. monel

12. The BEST flux to use for soldering galvanized iron is   12.____

     A. resin   B. sal ammoniac
     C. borax   D. muriatic acid

13. The one of the following that is NOT a common type of oilstone is   13.____

     A. silicon carbide   B. aluminum oxide
     C. hard Arkansas   D. pumice

14. A method of joining metals using temperatures intermediate between soldering and welding is   14.____

     A. corbelling   B. brazing   C. annealing   D. lapping

15. When an unusually high degree of accuracy is required with woodwork, lines should be marked with a   15.____

     A. pencil ground to a chisel point
     B. pencil line over a crayon line
     C. sharp knife point
     D. scriber

16. The MOST important difference between pipe threads and V threads on bolts is that pipe threads are usually   16.____

     A. longer   B. sharper
     C. tapered   D. more evenly spaced

17. A street elbow differs from the ordinary elbow in that the street elbow has   17.____

     A. different diameter threads at each end
     B. male threads at one end and female threads at the other
     C. female threads at both ends
     D. male threads at both ends

18. Water hammer in a pipe line can MOST often be stopped by the installation of a(n)   18.____

     A. pressure reducing valve   B. expansion joint
     C. flexible coupling   D. air chamber

19. If water is leaking from the top part of a bibcock, the part that should be replaced is MOST likely the   19.____

    A. bibb washer   B. packing
    C. seat   D. bibb screw

20. When joining electric wires together in a fixture box, the BEST thing to use are wire   20.____

    A. connectors   B. couplings   C. clamps   D. bolts

21. If the name plate of a motor indicates that it is a split phase motor, it is LIKELY that this motor   21.____

    A. is a universal motor
    B. operates on DC only
    C. operates on AC only
    D. operates either on DC at full power or on AC at reduced power

22. To make driving of a screw into hard wood easier, it is BEST to lubricate the threads of the screw with   22.____

    A. varnoline   B. penetrating oil
    C. beeswax   D. cutting oil

23. Assume that a thermostatically controlled oil heater fails to operate. To determine whether it is the thermostat that is at fault, you should   23.____

    A. check the circuit breaker
    B. connect a wire across the terminals of the thermostat
    C. replace the contacts on the thermostat
    D. put an ammeter on the line

24. The function of the carburetor on a gasoline engine is to   24.____

    A. mix the air and gasoline properly
    B. filter the fuel
    C. filter the air to engine
    D. pump the gasoline into the cylinder

25. If a car owner complains that the battery in his car is constantly running dry, the item that should be checked FIRST is the   25.____

    A. fan belt   B. generator
    C. voltage regulator   D. relay

26. On MOST modern automobiles, foot brake pressure is transmitted to the brake drums by   26.____

    A. air pressure   B. mechanical linkage
    C. hydraulic fluid   D. electro-magnetic force

27. Assume that the engine of a car remains cold even though it is run for a period of time. The part that is MOST likely at fault is the   27.____

    A. heat by-pass valve   B. thermostat
    C. heater control   D. choke

28. To permit easy stripping of concrete forms, they should be   28._____

    A. dried   B. oiled   C. wet down   D. cleaned

29. To prevent honey combing in concrete, the concrete should be   29._____

    A. vibrated   B. cured
    C. heated in cold weather   D. protected from the rain

30. The MAIN reason for using wire mesh in connection with concrete work is to   30._____

    A. strain the impurities from the sand
    B. increase the strength of the concrete
    C. hold the forms together
    D. protect the concrete till it hardens

31. Segregation of concrete is MOST often caused by pouring concrete   31._____

    A. in cold weather
    B. from too great a height
    C. too rapidly
    D. into a form in which the concrete has already begun to harden

32. Headers in carpentry are MOST closely associated with   32._____

    A. trimmers   B. cantilevers
    C. posts   D. newels

33. Joists are very often supported by   33._____

    A. suspenders   B. base plates
    C. anchor bolts   D. bridal irons

34. At outside corners, the type of joint MOST frequently used on a baseboard is the   34._____

    A. plowed   B. mitered
    C. mortise and tenon   D. butt

35. The vehicle used with latex paints is usually   35._____

    A. linseed oil   B. shellac
    C. varnish   D. water

36. *Boxing* of paint refers to the _____ of paints.   36._____

    A. mixing   B. storage   C. use   D. canning

37. When painting wood, nail holes should be puttied   37._____

    A. *before* applying the prime coat
    B. *after* applying the prime coat but before the second coat
    C. *after* applying the second coat but before the third coat
    D. *after* applying the third coat

38. In laying up a brick wall, you find that at the end of the wall there is not enough space for   38._____
a full brick.
You should use a

    A. stretcher   B. bat   C. corbel   D. bull nose

39. Pointing a brick wall is the same as   39.____

    A. truing up the wall
    B. topping the wall with a waterproof surface
    C. repairing the mortar joints in the wall
    D. providing a foundation for the wall

40. The pigment MOST often used in a prime coat of paint on steel to prevent rusting is   40.____

    A. lampblack   B. calcimine
    C. zinc oxide   D. red lead

41. If you find a co-worker lying unconscious across an electric wire, the FIRST thing you   41.____
should do is

    A. get him off the wire   B. call the foreman
    C. get a doctor   D. shut off the power

42.   42.____

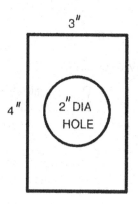

The area of the metal plate shown above, minus the hole area, is MOST NEARLY
_____ square inches.

    A. 8.5   B. 8.9   C. 9.4   D. 10.1

43.   43.____

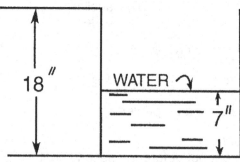

The percentage of the above tank that is filled with water is MOST NEARLY

    A. 33   B. 35   C. 37   D. 39

44.   44.____

TOP
VIEW

FRONT
VIEW

The top and front view of an object are shown above. The right side view will MOST likely look like

A.   B.   C.   D.

45.   45.____

The distance between centers of the holes in the above diagram is MOST NEARLY

A. $4\frac{1}{2}$"   B.   4 3/4"   C.   5"   D. $5\frac{1}{4}$"

Questions 46-48.

DIRECTIONS: Questions 46 through 48, inclusive, are to be answered in accordance with the paragraph below.

A steam heating system with steam having a pressure of less than 10 pounds is called a low-pressure system. The majority of steam-heating systems are of this type. The steam may be provided by low-pressure boilers installed _expressly_ for the purpose, or it may be gener-

89

ated in boilers at a higher pressure and reduced in pressure before admitted to the heating mains. In other instances, it may be possible to use exhaust steam which has been made to run engines and other machines and which still contains enough heat to be utilized in the heating system. The first case represents the system of heating used in the ordinary residence or other small building; the other two represent the systems of heating employed in industrial buildings where a power plant is installed for general power purposes.

46. According to the above paragraph, whether or not a steam heating system is considered a low pressure system is determined by the pressure

    46.____

    A.   generated by the boiler
    B.   in the heating main
    C.   at the inlet side of the reducing valve
    D.   of the exhaust

47. According to the above paragraph, steam used for heating is sometimes obtained from steam

    47.____

    A.   generated principally to operate machinery
    B.   exhausted from larger boilers
    C.   generated at low pressure and brought up to high pressure before being used
    D.   generated by engines other than boilers

48. As used in the above paragraph, the word *expressly* means

    48.____

    A.   rapidly   B.   specifically
    C.   usually   D.   mainly

49. Of the following words, the one that is CORRECTLY spelled is

    49.____

    A.   suficient   B.   sufficiant
    C.   sufficient   D.   suficiant

50. Of the following words, the one that is CORRECTLY spelled is

    50.____

    A.   fairly   B.   fairley   C.   farely   D.   fairlie

KEY (CORRECT ANSWERS)

1. B	11. B	21. C	31. B	41. D
2. A	12. D	22. C	32. A	42. B
3. A	13. D	23. B	33. D	43. D
4. C	14. B	24. A	34. B	44. A
5. C	15. C	25. C	35. D	45. C
6. C	16. C	26. C	36. A	46. B
7. B	17. B	27. B	37. B	47. A
8. A	18. D	28. B	38. B	48. B
9. C	19. B	29. A	39. C	49. C
10. B	20. A	30. B	40. D	50. A

EXAMINATION SECTION
TEST 1

DIRECTIONS: Each question or incomplete statement is followed by several suggested answers or completions. Select the one that BEST answers the question or completes the statement. *PRINT THE LETTER OF THE CORRECT ANSWER IN THE SPACE AT THE RIGHT.*

1. The composition of plumber's solder for wiping is APPROXIMATELY (ratio of tin to lead)   1.____

    A. 40-60   B. 50-50   C. 60-40   D. 70-30

2. A device used to lift sewage to the level of a sewer from a floor below the sewer grade is known as a(n)   2.____

    A. elevator   B. ejector   C. sump   D. conveyer

3. A check valve in a piping system will   3.____

    A. permit excessive pressures in a boiler
    B. eliminate water hammer
    C. permit water to flow in only one direction
    D. control the rate of flow of water

4. The chemical MOST frequently used to clean drains clogged with grease is   4.____

    A. muriatic acid   B. soda ash
    C. ammonia   D. caustic soda

5. To test for leaks in a newly installed C.I. waste stack,   5.____

    A. oil of peppermint is poured into the top of the stack
    B. smoke under pressure is pumped into the stack
    C. a water meter is used to measure the water flow
    D. dye is placed in the system at the top of the stack

6. When installing a catch basin, the outlet should be located   6.____

    A. at the same level as the inlet
    B. above the inlet
    C. below the inlet
    D. at the invert

7. The copper float in a low down water tank is perforated so that water enters the ball. As a result, the tank will   7.____

    A. flush once, and then will not operate again
    B. not flush at all
    C. not flush completely
    D. continue to flush, but water will be wasted

8. If water leaks from the stem of a faucet when the faucet is opened, the _____ should be   8.____

    A. faucet; replaced   B. cap nut; rethreaded
    C. seat; reground   D. packing; replaced

9. In a hot water heating system, it may be necessary to *bleed* radiators to
    9.__

    A. relieve high steam pressure
    B. permit entrapped, air to escape
    C. allow condensate to return to the boiler
    D. drain off waste water

10. When painting raw wood, puttying of nail holes should be done
    10.__

    A. 24 hours before the prime coat
    B. immediately before the prime coat
    C. after the prime coat and before the second coat
    D. after the second coat and before the finish

11. In general, the one of the following that will dry *tack free* in the SHORTEST time is
    11.__

    A. lacquer   B. varnish   C. enamel   D. oil paint

12. The *vehicle* MOST frequently used in paints for exterior wood surfaces is
    12.__

    A. white lead   B. linseed oil
    C. japan   D. varnish

13. Painting of an interior plastered wall is usually delayed until the plaster is dry.
    If this practice is NOT followed, the paint might
    13.__

    A. chalk   B. fade   C. run   D. blister

14. A *sealer* applied over knots and pitch streaks to prevent *bleeding* through paint is
    14.__

    A. shellac   B. lacquer
    C. coal tar   D. carnauba wax

15. Painting of outside steel in near freezing (32° F) weather is poor practice MAINLY
    because
    15.__

    A. the paint will not dry properly
    B. ice will form in the thinner
    C. more paint is required
    D. paint fumes are dangerous

16. When repainting exterior woodwork that has a glossy finish, good adhesion of paint is
    BEST obtained by first
    16.__

    A. *washing* the work with diluted lye
    B. *dulling* the work with sandpaper
    C. *warming* the work with an electric heater
    D. *roughening* the work with a rasp

17. The one of the following methods of cleaning steelwork prior to painting that is NOT com-
    monly used on exterior work, such as bridges, is
    17.__

    A. sandblasting   B. flame cleaning
    C. wire brushing   D. pickling

18. When spraying oil paints, the type of gun and nozzle preferred is a _____ feed gun, _____ mix nozzle.

    A. pressure; internal   B. pressure, external
    C. syphon; internal   D. syphon; external

18.____

19. When opening a bag of cement, you find that the cement is lumpy.
The cement should be

    A. discarded and not used at all
    B. crushed before placing in the mixer
    C. used as is since the mixer will grind it
    D. well mixed with water and stored overnight before using

19.____

20. A 1:2:4 concrete mix by volume is specified.
If 6 cubic feet of cement is to be used in the mix, the volume of sand to use is, in cubic feet,

    A. 3   B. 6   C. 12   D. 24

20.____

21. Honeycombing in concrete is BEST prevented by

    A. increasing water-cement ratio
    B. heating concrete in cold weather
    C. using mechanical vibrators
    D. adding calcium chloride

21.____

22. When a lightweight concrete is required, the one of the following that is COMMONLY used as an aggregate is

    A. gravel   B. brick chips   C. stone   D. cinders

22.____

23. A rubbed finish on concrete is USUALLY obtained by use of a

    A. carborundum brick   B. garnet sanding belt
    C. fibre brush and wax   D. pad of steel wool

23.____

24. A copper strip is frequently embedded in the concrete across a construction joint in a concrete wall.
The purpose of this is to

    A. make a watertight joint
    B. bond the two parts of the wall together
    C. prevent unequal settlement
    D. retard temperature cracking

24.____

25. In brickwork laid in common bond, a header course USUALLY occurs in every _____ course.

    A. 2nd   B. 4th   C. 6th   D. 8th

25.____

26. Pointing of brickwork refers to

    A. cutting brick to fit   B. patching mortar joints
    C. attaching brick veneer   D. arranging brick in an arch

26.____

27. Furring is applied to brick walls to 27.___

    A. strengthen the wall
    B. waterproof the wall
    C. provide ventilation to prevent condensation
    D. provide a base for lathing

28. The FIRST coat in plaster work is *scratched* in order to 28.___

    A. remove excess plaster
    B. smooth the base for the second coat
    C. provide a bond for the second coat
    D. strengthen the base coat

29. An alloy used where resistance to corrosion is important is 29.___

    A. tungsten   B. mild steel   C. monel   D. tin

30. The size of iron pipe is given in terms of its nominal 30.___

    A. weight   B. inside diameter
    C. outside diameter   D. wall thickness

31. When preparing surfaces to be soldered, the FIRST step is 31.___

    A. tinning   B. sweating   C. heating   D. cleaning

32. To test for leaks in an acetylene torch, it is BEST that one use 32.___

    A. soapy water   B. a match
    C. a gas with a strong odor   D. a pressure gauge

33. One advantage of using a Pittsburgh lock seam when joining two pieces of sheet metal is that, once formed in the shop, it may be assembled anywhere with a 33.___

    A. hickey   B. swage   C. template   D. mallet

34. White cast iron is 34.___

    A. hard and brittle   B. hard and ductile
    C. ductile and malleable   D. brittle and malleable

35. The gage used for measuring copper wire is 35.___

    A. U.S. Standard   B. Stubbs
    C. Washburn and Moen   D. Brown and Sharpe

36. The BEST flux to use when soldering copper wires in an electric circuit is 36.___

    A. sal ammoniac   B. zinc chloride
    C. rosin   D. borax

37. The spark test, to determine the approximate composition of an unknown metal, is made by 37.___

    A. holding the metal against a grinding wheel
    B. striking flint on the unknown metal
    C. connecting wires from a source of electric power to the metal and striking an arc with a bare wire
    D. heating with an oxyacetylene torch

38. The one of the following metals that is MOST commonly used for bearings is   38._____

    A. duraluminum   B. brass   C. babbit   D. lead

39. A *tailstock* is found on a   39._____

    A. drill press   B. shaper   C. planer   D. lathe

40. The BEST lubricant to use when cutting screw threads in steel is   40._____

    A. naphtha   B. 3-in-1 oil
    C. lard oil   D. linseed oil

41. When a high speed cutting tool is required, the tip is frequently made of   41._____

    A. carborundum   B. tungsten carbide
    C. bronze   D. vanadium

42. A nut is turned on a 3/4"-10 bolt.
When the nut is turned five complete turns on this bolt, the distance it moves along the bolt   42._____

    A. depends on the type of thread   B. is 0.2 inches
    C. is 0.375 inches   D. is 0.5 inches

43. Of the following, the STRONGEST screw thread form is the   43._____

    A. Whitworth   B. Acme
    C. National Standard   D. V

44. *Knurling* refers to   44._____

    A. rolling depressions in a fixed pattern on a cylindrical surface
    B. turning between centers on a lathe
    C. making deep cuts in a flat plate with a milling machine
    D. drilling matching holes in bolt and nut for a cotter pin

45. A special device used to guide the drill as well as to hold the work when drilling is known as a   45._____

    A. dolly   B. jig   C. chuck   D. collet

46. Tools that have a *Morse taper* would be used on a   46._____

    A. milling machine   B. shaper
    C. planer   D. drill press

47. When tapping a blind hole in a plate, the FIRST tap to use is a   47._____

    A. plug   B. bottoming   C. lead   D. taper

48. An important safety practice to remember when cutting a rivet with a chisel is to wear   48._____

    A. leather gloves   B. steel toe shoes
    C. cup goggles   D. a hard hat

49. Electricians working around *live wires* should wear gloves made of   49.____

    A. asbestos   B. metal mesh   C. leather   D. rubber

50. Storage of oily rags presents a safety hazard because of possible   50.____

    A. fire   B. poisonous flames
    C. attraction of rats   D. leakage of oil

———

KEY (CORRECT ANSWERS)

1.	A	11.	A	21.	C	31.	D	41.	B
2.	B	12.	B	22.	D	32.	A	42.	D
3.	C	13.	D	23.	A	33.	D	43.	B
4.	D	14.	A	24.	A	34.	A	44.	A
5.	B	15.	A	25.	C	35.	B	45.	B
6.	C	16.	B	26.	B	36.	C	46.	D
7.	D	17.	D	27.	D	37.	A	47.	D
8.	D	18.	A	28.	C	38.	C	48.	C
9.	B	19.	A	29.	C	39.	D	49.	D
10.	C	20.	C	30.	B	40.	C	50.	A

———

TEST 2

DIRECTIONS: Each question or incomplete statement is followed by several suggested answers or completions. Select the one that BEST answers the question or completes the statement. *PRINT THE LETTER OF THE CORRECT ANSWER IN THE SPACE AT THE RIGHT.*

1. *Shimmying* of the front wheels of a truck is MOST frequently caused by   1.____

    A. worn front brake drums   B. a worn differential gear
    C. a loose steering gear   D. a dead shock absorber

2. The MOST important reason for maintaining correct air pressure in all tires of a truck is to   2.____

    A. prevent the truck from swerving when brakes are applied
    B. permit the truck to stop quicker in an emergency
    C. provide a smoother ride
    D. prevent excessive wear on the tires

3. The oil gage on the dashboard of a truck indicates   3.____

    A. the amount of oil in the pan
    B. the pressure at which the oil is being pumped
    C. if the oil filter is working
    D. the temperature of the oil in the motor

4. An unbalanced wheel on a truck is corrected by   4.____

    A. bending the rim slightly
    B. adjusting the king pin
    C. changing the ratio of caster to camber
    D. adding small weights to the rim

5. A cold motor on a truck should be warmed up in wintertime by   5.____

    A. turning on the heater and pouring warm water into the radiator
    B. allowing the motor to idle for a few minutes
    C. racing the motor
    D. alternately pressing the gas pedal to the floor and releasing it

6. The brake pedal on a truck goes to the floorboard when pushed.   6.____
    The one of the following that would cause this condition is

    A. air in the hydraulic system
    B. wet brakes
    C. excessive fluid in the cylinders
    D. a loose backing plate

7. The ammeter of a truck indicates no charge during operation even though the battery is   7.____
    run down. To find the fault, the generator field terminal is grounded. The ammeter now
    shows a charge. The part that is defective is the

    A. generator field coil   B. armature
    C. brushes   D. voltage regulator

8. The part used to control the ratio of air and gasoline in a truck engine is the   8.___

    A. bogie   B. filter   C. carburetor   D. pump

9. The MAIN purpose of a vacuum booster on a truck engine is to   9.___

    A. increase the manifold vacuum
    B. assist windshield wiper operation
    C. provide a steadier fuel flow
    D. govern engine speed

10. The purpose of grounding the frame of an electric motor is to   10.___

    A. prevent excessive vibration   B. eliminate shock hazards
    C. reduce power requirements   D. prevent overheating

11. The one of the following that is NOT part of an electric motor is a   11.___

    A. brush   B. rheostat   C. pole   D. commutator

12. An electrical transformer would be used to   12.___

    A. change current from AC to DC   B. raise or lower the power
    C. raise or lower the voltage   D. change the frequency

13. The piece of equipment that would be rated in ampere hours is a   13.___

    A. storage battery   B. bus bar
    C. rectifier   D. capacitor

14. A ballast is a necessity in a(n)   14.___

    A. motor generator set   B. fluorescent lighting system
    C. oil circuit breaker   D. synchronous converter

15. The power factor in an AC circuit is on when   15.___

    A. no current is flowing
    B. the voltage at the source is a minimum
    C. the voltage and current are in phase
    D. there is no load

16.   16.___

Neglecting the internal resistance in the battery, the current flowing through the battery shown in the sketch above is _____ amp.

    A. 3   B. 6   C. 9   D. 12

17. When excess current flows, a circuit breaker is opened directly by the action of a   17._____

    A. condenser   B. transistor   C. relay   D. solenoid

18. The MAIN purpose of bridging in building floor construction is to   18._____

    A. spread floor loads evenly to joists
    B. reduce the number of joists required
    C. permit use of thinner subflooring
    D. reduce noise passage through floors

19. Of the following, the material MOST commonly used for subflooring is   19._____

    A. rock lath   B. insulation board
    C. plywood   D. transite

20. In connection with stair construction, the one of the following that is LEAST related to the   20._____
others is

    A. tread   B. cap   C. nosing   D. riser

21. The type of nail MOST commonly used in flooring is   21._____

    A. common   B. cut   C. brad   D. casing

22. The edge joint of flooring boards is COMMONLY   22._____

    A. mortise and tenon   B. shiplap
    C. half lap   D. tongue and groove

23. The purpose of a ridge board in building construction is to   23._____

    A. locate corners of a building
    B. keep plaster work smooth
    C. support the ends of roof rafters
    D. conceal openings at the eaves

24. To prevent splintering of wood when using an auger bit,   24._____

    A. the bit should be hollow ground
    B. hold the piece of wood in a vise
    C. clamp a piece of scrap wood to the back of the piece being drilled
    D. use a slow speed on the drill press

25. End grain of a post can be MOST easily planed by use of a _____ plane.   25._____

    A. rafter   B. jack   C. fore   D. block

26. A butt gauge is used when   26._____

    A. hanging doors   B. laying out stairs
    C. making rafter cuts   D. framing studs

27. The one of the following grades of sandpaper with the FINEST grit is   27._____

    A. 0   B. 2/0   C. 1/2   D. 1

28. The sum of the following numbers, 3 7/8, 14 1/4, 6 7/16, 22 3/16, 8 1/2 is   28.___

    A. 55 1/16   B. 55 1/8   C. 55 3/16   D. 55 1/4

29. The area of the rectangular field shown in the dia-   29.___
gram at the right is , in square feet,

    A. 29,456
    B. 29,626
    C. 29,716
    D. 29,836

437 FT.

68 ft

30. The cost of material is approximately 3/8ths of the total cost of a certain job.   30.___
If the total cost of the job is $127.56, then the cost of material is MOST NEARLY

    A. $47.83   B. $48.24   C. $48.65   D. $49.06

31. A blueprint is drawn to a scale of 1/4" = 1'0". A line on the blueprint that is not dimen-   31.___
sioned is measured with a ruler and found to be 3 3/8" long.
The length represented by this line is

    A. 13'2"   B. 13'4"   C. 13'6"   D. 13'8"

32. A maintainer, in repairing a brick wall, spends one-half hour getting materials, forty-three   32.___
minutes chipping and cleaning the wall, fifteen minutes mixing the mortar, and one hour
and twenty-seven minutes in applying the brick and finishing.
The total time spent on this repair job is _____ hours
_____ minute(s).

    A. 2; 45   B. 2; 50   C. 2; 55   D. 3; 0

33. *Employees are responsible for the good care, proper maintenance, and serviceable con-*   33.___
dition of property issued or assigned to their use.
As used above, *serviceable condition* means MOST NEARLY

    A. capable of being repaired   B. fit for use
    C. ease of handling   D. minimum cost

34. An employee shall be on the alert constantly for potential accident hazards.   34.___
As used above, *potential* means MOST NEARLY

    A. dangerous   B. careless   C. possible   D. frequent

Questions 35-37.

DIRECTIONS: Questions 35 to 37, inclusive, are to be answered in accordance with the following paragraph.

    All cement work contracts, more or less, in setting. The contraction in concrete walls and
other structures causes fine cracks to develop at regular intervals. The tendency to contract
increases in direct proportion to the quantity of cement in the concrete. A rich mixture will
contract more than a lean mixture. A concrete wall, which has been made of a very lean mix-
ture and which has been built by filling only about one foot in depth of concrete in the form
each day will frequently require close inspection to reveal the cracks.

35. According to the above paragraph,   35.____

    A. shrinkage seldom occurs in concrete
    B. shrinkage occurs only in certain types of concrete
    C. by placing concrete at regular intervals, shrinkage may be avoided
    D. it is impossible to prevent shrinkage

36. According to the above paragraph, the one of the factors which reduces shrinkage in   36.____
concrete is the

    A. volume of concrete in wall
    B. height of each day's pour
    C. length of wall
    D. length and height of wall

37. According to the above paragraph, a rich mixture   37.____

    A. pours the easiest
    B. shows the largest amount of cracks
    C. is low in cement content
    D. need not be inspected since cracks are few

Questions 38-39.

DIRECTIONS: Questions 38 and 39 are to be answered in accordance with the following
paragraph.

*Painting is done to preserve surfaces, and unless the surface is properly prepared, good
preservation will not be possible. Apply paint only to clean dry surfaces. After a surface has
been scaled, which means that all loose paint and rust are removed by chipping, scraping,
and wire brushing, be sure all dust and dirt are completely removed.*

38. According to the above paragraph, the MAIN purpose of painting a wall is to _____ the   38.____
wall.

    A. clean   B. waterproof
    C. protect   D. remove dust from

39. According to the above paragraph,   39.____

    A. chipping, scraping, and wire brushing are the only methods permitted for cleaning
surfaces
    B. painting is effective only when the surface is clean
    C. scaling refers only to the removal of rust
    D. paint may be applied on wet surfaces

40. The order in which the dimensions of stock are listed on a bill of materials is   40.____

    A. thickness, length, and width   B. thickness, width, and length
    C. width, length, and thickness   D. length, thickness, and width

41. The glue that will BEST withstand extreme exposure to moisture and water is _____ glue.

    A. polyvinyl   B. resorcinol
    C. powdered resin   D. protein

41.___

42. Four board feet of lumber, listed at $350.00 per M, will cost

    A. $3.50   B. $1.40   C. $1.30   D. $4.00

42.___

43. The cap iron or chip breaker stiffens the plane iron and

    A. protects the cutting edge
    B. curls the shaving
    C. regulates the thickness of the shaving
    D. reduces mouth gap

43.___

44. Coping-saw blades have teeth shaped like those on a _____ saw.

    A. dovetail   B. crosscut   C. back   D. rip

44.___

45. Of the following, the claw hammer that is BEST suited for general use in a woodworking shop is the _____ claw.

    A. straight   B. bell-faced curved
    C. plain-faced curved   D. adze eye curved

45.___

46. The natural binder which cements wood fibers together and makes wood solid is

    A. cellulose   B. lignin
    C. alpha-cellulose   D. trichocarpa

46.___

47. The plane that is BEST suited for trimming the bottom of a dado or lap joint is the _____ plane.

    A. block   B. router   C. rabbet   D. core-box

47.___

48. Brads are fasteners that are similar to _____ nails.

    A. escutcheon   B. box
    C. finishing   D. duplex head

48.___

49. The plane in which the plane iron is inserted with its bevel in the up position is the _____ plane.

    A. fore   B. rabbet   C. block   D. circular

49.___

50. Coating materials used to protect wood against fire USUALLY contain a water soluble fire-retardant such as

    A. ammonium chloride   B. sodium perborate
    C. sodium silicate   D. sal soda

50.___

KEY (CORRECT ANSWERS)

1.	C	11.	B	21.	B	31.	C	41.	B
2.	D	12.	C	22.	D	32.	C	42.	B
3.	B	13.	A	23.	C	33.	B	43.	B
4.	D	14.	B	24.	C	34.	C	44.	D
5.	B	15.	C	25.	D	35.	D	45.	B
6.	A	16.	A	26.	A	36.	B	46.	B
7.	D	17.	D	27.	B	37.	B	47.	B
8.	C	18.	A	28.	D	38.	C	48.	C
9.	B	19.	C	29.	C	39.	B	49.	C
10.	B	20.	B	30.	A	40.	B	50.	C

———

ARITHMETICAL REASONING

EXAMINATION SECTION
TEST 1

DIRECTIONS: Each question or incomplete statement is followed by several suggested answers or completions. Select the one that BEST answers the question or completes the statement. *PRINT THE LETTER OF THE CORRECT ANSWER IN THE SPACE AT THE RIGHT.*

1. If it takes 2 men 9 days to do a job, how many men are needed to do the same job in 3 days?   1.____

    A. 4   B. 5   C. 6   D. 7

2. Suppose that a department operates 1,644 buildings. If one employee is needed for every 2 buildings, and one foreman is needed for every 18 employees, the number of foremen needed is CLOSEST to   2.____

    A. 45   B. 50   C. 55   D. 60

3. If 60 bars of soap cost the same as 2 gallons of wax, how many bars of soap can be bought for the price of 5 gallons of wax?   3.____

    A. 120   B. 150   C. 180   D. 300

4. An employee waxes 275 sq.ft. of floor on Monday, 352 sq.ft. on Tuesday, 179 sq.ft. on Wednesday, and 302 sq.ft. on Thursday.
In order to average 280 sq.ft. of floor waxed a day, how many square feet of floor must he wax on Friday?   4.____

    A. 264   B. 278   C. 292   D. 358

5. A project covers 35 acres altogether. Lawns, playgrounds, and walks take up 28 acres and the rest is given over to buildings.
What percentage of the total area is given over to buildings?   5.____

    A. 7%   B. 20%   C. 25%   D. 28%

6. When preparing for a mopping operation, fill the standard 16 quart bucket to the 3/4 full mark with warm water. Then add detergent at the rate of 2 oz. per gallon of water and disinfectant at the rate of 1 oz. to 3 gallons of water. According to these directions, the amount of detergent and disinfectant to add to 3/4 of a bucket of warm water is _____ oz. detergent and _____ oz. disinfectant.   6.____

    A. 4; 1/2   B. 5; 3/4   C. 6; 1   D. 8; 1 1/4

7. If corn brooms weigh 32 lbs. a dozen, the average weight of one corn broom is CLOSEST to _____ lbs. _____ oz.   7.____

    A. 2; 14   B. 2; 11   C. 2; 9   D. 2; 6

8. At the beginning of the year, a foreman has 7 dozen electric bulbs in stock. During the year, he receives a shipment of 14 dozen bulbs, and also replaces 5 burned out bulbs a month in each of 3 buildings in his area. How many electric bulbs does he have on hand at the end of the year? _____dozen.

    A. 3   B. 6   C. 8   D. 12

8.____

9. A project has 4 buildings, each 14 floors high. Each floor has 10 apartments. If 35% of the apartments in the project have 3 rooms or less, how many apartments have 4 or more rooms?

    A. 196   B. 210   C. 364   D. 406

9.____

10. An employee takes 1 hour and 30 minutes a day to sweep 30 flights of stairs. How many flights of stairs does he sweep in a month if he spends a total of 30 hours doing this job and works at the same rate?

    A. 200   B. 300   C. 600   D. 900

10.____

11. During a month, Employee A washed 30 windows, Employee B washed 4 times as many windows as Employee A, and Employee C washed half as many windows as Employee B. The TOTAL number of windows washed by all three men together during this month is

    A. 180   B. 210   C. 240   D. 330

11.____

12. How much would it cost to completely fence in the playground area shown at the right with fencing costing $7.50 a foot?
    A. $615.00
    B. $820.00
    C. $885.00
    D. $960.00

12.____

13. A drill bit measures .625 inches. The fractional equivalent, in inches, is

    A. 9/16   B. 5/8   C. 11/16   D. 3/4

13.____

14. The number of cubic yards of sand required to fill a bin measuring 12 feet by 6 feet by 4 feet is MOST NEARLY

    A. 8   B. 11   C. 48   D. 96

14.____

15. Assume that you are assigned to put down floor tiles in a room measuring 8 feet by 10 feet. Individual tiles measure 9 inches by 9 inches.
The total number of floor tiles required to cover the entire floor is MOST NEARLY

    A. 107   B. 121   C. 142   D. 160

15.____

16. Lumber is usually sold by the board foot, and a board foot is defined as a board one foot   16.____
square and one inch thick.
If the price of one board foot of lumber is 90 cents and you need 20 feet of lumber 6
inches wide and 1 inch thick, the cost of the 20 feet of lumber is

    A. $9.00   B. $12.00   C. $18.00   D. $24.00

17. For a certain plumbing repair job, you need three lengths of pipe, 12 1/4 inches, 6 1/2   17.____
inches, and 8 5/8 inches.
If you cut these three lengths from the same piece of pipe, which is 36 inches long,
and each cut consumes 1/8 inch of pipe, the length of pipe REMAINING after you have
cut out your three pieces should be _____ inches.

    A. 7 1/4   B. 7 7/8   C. 8 1/4   D. 8 7/8

18. A maintenance bond for a roadway pavement is in an amount of 10% of the estimated   18.____
cost.
If the estimated cost is $8,000,000, the maintenance bond is

    A. $8,000   B. $80,000   C. $800,000   D. $8,000,000

19. Specifications require that a core be taken every 700 square yards of paved roadway or   19.____
fraction thereof. A 100 foot by 200 foot rectangular area would require _____ core(s).

    A. 1   B. 2   C. 3   D. 4

20. An applicant must file a map at a scale of 1" = 40'. Six inches on the map represents   20.____
_____ feet on the ground.

    A. 600   B. 240   C. 120   D. 60

21. A 100' x 110' lot has an area of MOST NEARLY _____ acre.   21.____

    A. 1/8   B. 1/4   C. 3/8   D. 1/2

22. 1 inch is MOST NEARLY equal to _____ feet.   22.____

    A. .02   B. .04   C. .06   D. .08

23. The area of the triangle EFG shown   23.____
at the right is MOST NEARLY _____ sq. ft.

    A. 36   B. 42   C. 48   D. 54

24. Specifications state: As further security for the faithful performance of this contract, the   24.____
Comptroller shall deduct, and retain until the final payment, 10% of the value of the work
certified for payment in each partial payment voucher, until the amount so deducted and
retained shall equal 5% of the contract price or in the case of a unit price contract, 5% of
the estimated amount to be paid to the Contractor under the contract.
For a $300,000 contract, the amount to be retained at the end of the contract is

    A. $5,000   B. $10,000   C. $15,000   D. $20,000

25. Asphalt was laid for a length of 210 feet on the entire width of a street whose curb-to-curb   25.____
distance is 30 feet. The number of square yards covered with asphalt is MOST NEARLY

    A. 210   B. 700   C. 2,100   D. 6,300

KEY (CORRECT ANSWERS)

1.	C		11.	B
2.	A		12.	C
3.	B		13.	B
4.	C		14.	B
5.	B		15.	C
6.	C		16.	A
7.	B		17.	C
8.	B		18.	C
9.	C		19.	D
10.	C		20.	B

21.	B
22.	D
23.	A
24.	C
25.	B

SOLUTIONS TO PROBLEMS

1. $(2)(9) = 18$ man-days. Then, $18 \div 3 = 6$ men

2. The number of employees = $1644 \div 2 = 822$. The number of foremen needed
    $= 822 \div 18 \approx 45$

3. 1 gallon of wax costs the same as $60 \div 2 = 30$ bars of soap. Thus, 5 gallons of wax costs
    the same as $(5)(30) = 150$ bars of soap.

4. To average 280 sq.ft. for five days means a total of $(5)(280) = 1400$ sq.ft. for all five days.
    The number of square feet to be waxed on Friday = $1400 - (275+352+179+302) = 292$

5. The acreage for buildings is $35 - 28 = 7$. Then, $7/35 = 20\%$

6. $(16)(3/4) = 12$ quarts = 3 gallons. The amount of detergent, in ounces, is $(2)(3) = 6$. The
    amount of disinfectant is 1 oz.

7. One corn broom weighs $32 \div 12 = 2\ 2/3$ lbs. $\approx$ 2 lbs. 11 oz.

8. Number of bulbs at the beginning of the year = $(7)(12) + (14)(12) = 252$. Number of bulbs
    replaced over an entire year = $(5)(3)(12) = 180$. The number of unused bulbs = $252 - 180$
    $= 72 = 6$ dozen.

9. Total number of apartments = $(4)(14)(10) = 560$. The number of apartments with at least
    4 rooms = $(.65)(560) = 364$.

10. $30 \div 1\ 1/2 = 20$. Then, $(20)(30) = 600$ flights of stairs

11. The number of windows washed by A, B, C were 30, 120, and 60. Their total is 210.

12. The two missing dimensions are $26 - 14 = 12$ ft. and $33 - 9 = 24$ ft. Perimeter = $9 + 12 +$
    $33 + 26 + 24 + 14 = 118$ ft. Thus, total cost of fencing = $(118)(\$7.50) = \$885.00$

13. $.625 = \dfrac{625}{1000} = \dfrac{5}{8}$

14. $(12)(6)(4) = 288$ cu.ft. Now, 1 cu.yd. = 27 cu.ft.; 288 cu.ft. is equivalent to $10\ 2/3$ or about
    11 cu.yds.

15. 144 sq.in. = 1 sq.ft. The room measures (8 ft.)x(10 ft.) = 80 sq.ft. = 11,520 sq.in. Each tile
    measures $(9)(9) = 81$ sq.in. The number of tiles needed = $11,520 \div 81 = 142.2$ or about
    142.

16. 20 ft. by 6 in. = (20 ft.)(1/2 ft.) = 10 sq.ft. Then, $(10 \times .90) = \$9.00$

17. There will be 3 cuts in making 3 lengths of pipe, and these 3 cuts will use $(3)(1/8) = 3/8$
    in. of pipe. The amount of pipe remaining after the 3 pieces are removed = $36 - 12\ 1/4$
    $- 6\ 1/2 - 8\ 5/8 - 3/8 = 8\ 1/4$ in.

18. The maintenance bond = $(.10)(\$8,000,000) = \$800,000$

19. (100)(200) = 20,000 sq.ft. = 20,000 ÷ 9 ≈ 2222 sq.yds. Then, 2222 ÷ 700 ≈ 3.17. Since a core must be taken for each 700 sq.yds. plus any left over fraction, 4 cores will be needed.

20. Six inches means (6)(40) = 240 ft. of actual length.

21. (100 ft.)(110 ft.) = 11,000 sq.ft. ≈ 1222 sq.yds. Then, since 1 acre = 4840 sq.yds., 1222 sq.yds. is equivalent to about 1/4 acre.

22. 1 in. = 1/12 ft. ≈ .08 ft.

23. Area of $\triangle$ EFG = (1/2)(8)(6) + (1/2)(4)(6) = 36 sq.ft.

24. The amount to be retained = (.05)($300,000) = $15,000

25. (210)(30) = 6300 sq.ft. Since 1 sq.yd. = 9 sq.ft., 6300 sq.ft. equals 700 sq.yds.

———

TEST 2

DIRECTIONS: Each question or incomplete statement is followed by several suggested answers or completions. Select the one that BEST answers the question or completes the statement. *PRINT THE LETTER OF THE CORRECT ANSWER IN THE SPACE AT THE RIGHT.*

1. The TOTAL length of four pieces of 2" pipe, whose lengths are 7'3 1/2", 4'2 3/16", 5'7 5/16", and 8'5 7/8", respectively, is

    A. 24'6 3/4"   B. 24'7 15/16"
    C. 25'5 13/16"   D. 25'6 7/8"

1.____

2. Under the same conditions, the group of pipes that gives the SAME flow as one 6" pipe is (neglecting friction) _____ pipes.

    A. 3 3"   B. 4 3"   C. 2 4"   D. 3 4"

2.____

3. A water storage tank measures 5' long, 4' wide, and 6' deep and is filled to the 5 1/2' mark with water.
If one cubic foot of water weighs 62 pounds, the number of pounds of water required to COMPLETELY fill the tank is

    A. 7,440   B. 6,200   C. 1,240   D. 620

3.____

4. A hot water line made of copper has a straight horizontal run of 150 feet and, when installed, is at a temperature of 45°F. In use, its temperature rises to 190°F.
If the coefficient of expansion for copper is 0.0000095" per foot per degree F, the total expansion, in inches, in the run of pipe is given by the product of 150 multiplied by 0.0000095 by

    A. 145   B. 145 x 12
    C. 145 divided by 12   D. 145 x 12 x 12

4.____

5. To dig a trench 3'0" wide, 50'0" long, and 5'6" deep, the total number of cubic yards of earth to be removed is MOST NEARLY

    A. 30   B. 90   C. 140   D. 825

5.____

6. If it costs $65 for 20 feet of subway rail, the cost of 150 feet of this rail will be

    A. $487.50   B. $512.00   C. $589.50   D. $650.00

6.____

7. The number of cubic feet of concrete it takes to fill a form 10 feet long, 3 feet wide, and 6 inches deep is

    A. 12   B. 15   C. 20   D. 180

7.____

8. The sum of 4 1/16, 51/4, 3 5/8, and 4 7/16 is

    A. 17 3/16   B. 17 1/4   C. 17 5/16   D. 17 3/8

8.____

9. If you earn $10.20 per hour and time and one-half for working over 40 hours, your gross salary for a week in which you worked 42 hours would be

    A. $408.00   B. $428.40   C. $438.60   D. $770.80

9.____

10. A drill bit, used to drill holes in track ties, has a diameter of 0.75 inches. When expressed as a fraction, the diameter of this drill bit is

    A. 1/4"   B. 3/8"   C. 1/2"   D. 3/4"

10.____

11. Three dozen shovels were purchased for use. If the shovels were used at the rate of nine a week, the number of weeks that the three dozen lasted was

    A. 3   B. 4   C. 9   D. 12

11.____

12. Assume that you earn $20,000 per year. If twenty percent of your pay is deducted for taxes, social security, and pension, your weekly take-home pay will be MOST NEARLY

    A. $280   B. $308   C. $328   D. $344

12.____

13. If a measurement scaled from a drawing is one inch, and the scale of the drawing is 1/8 inch to the foot, then the one inch measurement would represent an ACTUAL length of

    A. 8 feet   B. 2 feet
    C. 1/8 of a foot   D. 8 inches

13.____

14. Tiles 12" x 12" are used to lay a floor having the dimensions 10'0" x 12'0". The MINIMUM number of tiles needed to completely cover the floor is

    A. 60   B. 96   C. 120   D. 144

14.____

15. The volume of concrete in a strip of sidewalk 30 feet long by 4 feet wide by 3 inches thick is _____ cubic feet.

    A. 30   B. 120   C. 240   D. 360

15.____

16. To change a quantity of cubic feet into an equivalent quantity of cubic yards, _____ the quantity by _____.

    A. multiply; 9   B. divide; 9
    C. multiply; 27   D. divide; 27

16.____

17. If a pump can deliver 50 gallons of water per minute, then the time needed for this pump to empty an excavation containing 5,800 gallons of water is _____ hour(s) _____ minutes.

    A. 2; 12   B. 1; 56   C. 1; 44   D. 1; 32

17.____

18. The sum of 3 1/6", 4 1/4", 3 5/8", and 5 7/16" is

    A. 15 9/16"   B. 16 1/8"   C. 16 23/48"   D. 16 3/4"

18.____

19. If a measurement scaled from a drawing is 2 inches, and the scale of the drawing is 1/8 inch to the foot, then the two inch measurement would represent an ACTUAL length of

    A. 8 feet   B. 4 feet
    C. 1/4 of a foot   D. 16 feet

19.____

20. A room is 7'6" wide by 9'0" long with a ceiling height of 8'0". One gallon of flat paint will cover approximately 400 square feet of wall.
The number of gallons of this paint required to paint the walls of this room, making no deductions for windows or doors, is MOST NEARLY

20.____

    A. 1/4   B. 1/2   C. 2/3   D. 1

21. The cost of a certain job is broken down as follows:

21.____

        Materials $3,750
        Rental of equipment   1,200
        Labor   3,150

The percentage of the total cost of the job that can be charged to materials is MOST NEARLY

    A. 40%   B. 42%   C. 44%   D. 46%

22. By trial, it is found that by using two cubic feet of sand, a 5 cubic foot batch of concrete is produced. Using the same proportions, the amount of sand required
to produce 2 cubic yards of concrete is MOST NEARLY _____ cubic feet.

22.____

    A. 20   B. 22   C. 24   D. 26

23. It takes 4 men 6 days to do a certain job.
Working at the same speed, the number of days it will take 3 men to do this job is

23.____

    A. 7   B. 8   C. 9   D. 10

24. The cost of rawl plugs is $27.50 per gross. The cost of 2,448 rawl plugs is

24.____

    A. $467.50   B. $472.50   C. $477.50   D. $482.50

25. In a certain district, the area of a building may be no longer than 55% of the area of the lot on which it stands. On a rectangular lot 75 ft. by 125 ft., the maximum permissible area of building is, in square feet, MOST NEARLY

25.____

    A. 5,148   B. 5,152   C. 5,156   D. 5,160

KEY (CORRECT ANSWERS)

1.	D	11.	B
2.	B	12.	B
3.	D	13.	A
4.	A	14.	C
5.	A	15.	A
6.	A	16.	D
7.	B	17.	B
8.	D	18.	C
9.	C	19.	D
10.	D	20.	C

21.	D
22.	B
23.	B
24.	A
25.	C

———

SOLUTIONS TO PROBLEMS

1. $3\frac{1}{6}"+4\frac{1}{4}"+3\frac{5}{8}"+5\frac{7}{16}"+=3\frac{8}{48}"+4\frac{12}{48}"+3\frac{30}{48}"+5\frac{21}{48}"=15\frac{71}{48}"=16\frac{23}{48}"$

2. The flow of a 6" pipe is measured by the cross-sectional area. Since diameter = 6", radius = 3", and so area = 9 π sq.in. A single 3" pipe would have a cross-sectional area of (3/2) π sq.in. = 2.25 π sq.in. Now, 9 ÷ / 2.25 = 4. Thus, four 3" pipes is equivalent, in flow, to one 6" pipe.

3. (5x4x6) - (5x4x5 1/2) = 10. Then, (10)(62) = 620 pounds.

4. The total expansion = (150')(.0000095"/1 ft.)(190°-45°). So, the last factor is 145.

5. (3')(50')(5 1/2') = 825 cu.ft. Since 1 cu.yd. = 27 cu.ft., 825 cu.ft. cu.yds.

6. 150 ÷ 20 = 7.5. Then, (7.5)($65) = $487.50

7. (10')(3')(1/2') = 15 cu.ft.

8. $4\frac{1}{16}+5\frac{4}{16}+3\frac{10}{16}+4\frac{7}{16}=16\frac{22}{16}=17\frac{3}{8}$

9. Gross salary = ($10.20)(40) + ($15.30)(2) = $438.60

10. $75"=\frac{75}{100}"=\frac{3}{4}"$

11. 3 dozen = 36 shovels. Then, 36 ÷ 9 = 4 weeks

12. Since 20% is deducted, the take-home pay = ($20,000)(.80) = $16,000 for the year, which is $16,000 ÷ 52 ≈ $308 per week.

13. A scale drawing where 1/8" means an actual size of 1 ft. implies that a scale drawing of 1" means an actual size of (1')(8) = 8'

14. (10')(12') = 120 sq.ft. Since each tile is 1 sq.ft., a total of 120 tiles will be used.

15. (30')(4')(1/4') = 30 cu.ft.

16. To convert a given number of cubic feet into an equivalent number of cubic yards, divide by 27.

17. 5800 ÷ 50 = 116 min. = 1 hour 56 minutes

18. $3\frac{1}{6}"+4\frac{1}{4}"+3\frac{5}{8}"+5\frac{7}{16}"+=3\frac{8}{48}"+4\frac{12}{48}"+3\frac{30}{48}"+5\frac{21}{48}"=15\frac{71}{48}"=16\frac{23}{48}"$

19. 2 ÷ 1/8 = 16, so a 2" drawing represents an actual length of 16 feet.

20. The area of the 4 walls = 2(7 1/2')(8') + 2(9')(8') = 264 sq.ft. Then, 264 ÷ 400 = .66 or about 2/3 gallon of paint.

21. $3750 + $1200 + $3150 = $8100. Then, $3750/$8100 ≈ 46%

22. 2 cu.yds. ÷ 5 cu.ft. = 54 ÷ 5 = 10.8. Now, (10.8)(2 cu.ft.) ≈ 22 cu.ft. Note: 2 cu.yds. = 54 cu.ft.

23. (4)(6) = 24 man-days. Then, 24 ÷ 3 = 8 days

24. 2448 ÷ 144 = 17. Then, (17)($27.50) = $467.50

25. (75')(125') = 9375 sq.ft. The maximum area of the building = (.55)(9375 sq.ft.) * 5156 sq.ft.

TEST 3

DIRECTIONS: Each question or incomplete statement is followed by several suggested answers or completions. Select the one that BEST answers the question or completes the statement. *PRINT THE LETTER OF THE CORRECT ANSWER IN THE SPACE AT THE RIGHT.*

1. A steak weighed 2 pounds, 4 ounces.
   How much did it cost at $4.60 per pound?

   A. $7.80   B. $8.75   C. $9.90   D. $10.35

   1.____

2. twenty pints of water just fill a pail.
   the capacity of the pail, in gallons, is

   A. 2   B. 2 1/4   C. 2 1/2   D. 2 3/4

   2.____

3. The sum of 5/12 and 1/4 is

   A. 7/12   B. 2/3   C. 3/4   D. 5/6

   3.____

4. The volume of earth, in cubic yards, excavated from a trench 4'0" wide by 5'6" deep by 18'6" long is MOST NEARLY

   A. 14.7   B. 15.1   C. 15.5   D. 15.9

   4.____

5. 5/8 written as a decimal is

   A. 62.5   B. 6.25   C. .625   D. .0625

   5.____

6. The number of cubic feet in a cubic yard is

   A. 9   B. 12   C. 27   D. 36

   6.____

7. If it costs $16.20 to lay one square yard of asphalt, to lay a patch 15' by 15', it will cost MOST NEARLY

   A. $405.00   B. $3,645.00   C. $134.50   D. $243.00

   7.____

8. You are assigned thirty (30) asphalt workers to be divided into two crews so that one crew will have 2/3 as many men as the other.
   The number of men you would put into the SMALLER crew is

   A. 10   B. 12   C. 14   D. 20

   8.____

9. It takes 12 asphalt workers, working 6 hours a day, 5 days to complete a certain job.
   The number of days it will take 10 men, working 8 hours a day, to do the same job, assuming all work at the same rate, is

   A. 2 1/2   B. 3   C. 4 1/2   D. 6

   9.____

0. A street is laid to a 3% grade.
   This means that in 150 ft., the street grade will rise

   A. 4 1/2 inches   B. 45 inches
   C. 4 1/2 feet   D. 45 feet

   10.____

11. The sum of the following dimensions, 3 4/8, 4 1/8, 5 1/8, and 6 1/4, is   11._____

    A. 19   B. 19 1/8   C. 19 1/4   D. 19 1/2

12. A worker is paid $9.30 per hour.   12._____
If he works 8 hours each day on Monday, Tuesday, and Wednesday, 3 1/2 hours on
Thursday, and 3 hours on Friday, the TOTAL amount due him is

    A. $283.65   B. $289.15   C. $276.20   D. $285.35

13. The price of metal lath is $395.00 per 100 square yards. The cost of 527 square yards of   13._____
this lath is MOST NEARLY

    A. $2,076.50   B. $2,079.10   C. $2,081.70   D. $2,084.30

14. The total cost of applying 221 square yards of plaster board is $3,430.   14._____
The cost per square yard is MOST NEARLY

    A. $14.00   B. $14.50   C. $15.00   D. $15.50

15. In a three-coat plaster job, the scratch coat is 1/8 in. thick in front of the lath, the brown   15._____
coat is 3/16 in. thick, and the finish coat is 1/8 in. thick.
The TOTAL thickness of this plaster job, measured from the face of the lath, is

    A. 7/16"   B. 1/2"   C. 9/16"   D. 5/8"

16. If an asphalt worker earns $38,070 per year, his wages per month are MOST NEARLY   16._____

    A. $380.70   B. $735.00   C. $3,170.00   D. $3,807.00

17. The sum of 4 1/2 inches, 3 1/4 inches, and 7 1/2 inches is 1 foot _____ inches.   17._____

    A. 3   B. 3 1/4   C. 3 1/2   D. 4

18. The area of a rectangular asphalt patch, 9 ft. 3 in. by 6 ft. 9 in., is _____square feet.   18._____

    A. 54   B. 54 1/4   C. 54 1/2   D. 62 7/16

19. The number of cubic feet in a cubic yard is   19._____

    A. 3   B. 9   C. 16   D. 27

20. A 450 ft. long street with a grade of 2% will have one end of the street higher than the   20._____
other end by _____ feet.

    A. 2   B. 44   C. 9   D. 20

21. If the drive wheel of a roller is 6 ft. in diameter and the tiller wheel is 4 ft. in diameter,   21._____
whenever the drive wheel makes a complete revolution on a straight pass, the tiller wheel
makes _____ revolution(s).

    A. 1   B. 1 1/4   C. 1 1/2   D. 2

22. A point on the centerline of a street is marked: Station 42 + 51. Another point on the cen-   22._____
terline 30 feet from the first is marked Station 42+81.
A third should be marked Station

    A. 12+51   B. 42+21   C. 45+51   D. 72+51

23. In twenty minutes, a truck moving with a speed of 30 miles an hour will cover a distance   23.____
    of _____ miles.

    A. 3   B. 5   C. 10   D. 30

24. The number of pounds in a ton is   24.____

    A. 500   B. 1,000   C. 2,000   D. 5,000

25. During his summer vacation, a boy earned $45.00 per day and saved 60% of his earn-   25.____
    ings.
    If he worked 45 days, how much did he save during his vacation?

    A. $15.00   B. $18.00   C. $1,215.00   D. $22.50

KEY (CORRECT ANSWERS)

1.	D		11.	A
2.	C		12.	A
3.	B		13.	C
4.	B		14.	D
5.	C		15.	A
6.	C		16.	C
7.	A		17.	B
8.	B		18.	D
9.	C		19.	D
10.	C		20.	C

21.	C
22.	B
23.	C
24.	C
25.	C

SOLUTIONS TO PROBLEMS

1. ($4.60)(2 1/4 lbs.) = $10.35

2. 1 gallon = 8 pints, so 20 pints = 20/8 = 2 1/2 gallons

3. $\dfrac{5}{12}+\dfrac{1}{4}=\dfrac{5}{12}+\dfrac{3}{12}=\dfrac{8}{12}=\dfrac{2}{3}$

4. (4')(5 1/2')(18 1/2') = 407 cu.ft. Since 1 cu.yd. = 27 cu.ft., 407 cu.ft. $\approx$ 15.1 cu.yds.

5. 5/8=5 ÷ 8.000 = .625

6. There are (3)(3)(3) =27 cu.ft. in a cu.yd.

7. (15')(15') = 225 sq.ft. = 25 sq.yds. Then, ($16.20)(25) = $405.00

8. Let 2x = size of smaller crew and 3x = size of larger crew. Then, 2x + 3x = 30. Solving, x = 6. Thus, the smaller crew consists of 12 workers.

9. (12)(6)(5) = 360 worker-days. Then, 360 ÷ [(10)(8)] = 4 1/2 days

10. (.03)(150') = 4 1/2 ft.

11. $3\dfrac{4}{8}+4\dfrac{1}{8}+5\dfrac{1}{8}+6\dfrac{2}{8}=18\dfrac{8}{8}=19$

12. ($9.30)(8+8+8+3 1/2+3) = ($9.30)(30 1/2) = $283.65

13. The cost of 527 sq.yds. = (5.27)($395.00) = $2081.65 $\approx$ $2081.70

14. $3430 ÷ 221 $\approx$ $15.50

15. $\dfrac{1}{8}"+\dfrac{3}{16}"+\dfrac{1}{8}"=\dfrac{2}{16}"+\dfrac{3}{16}"+\dfrac{2}{16}"=\dfrac{7}{16}"$

16. $38,070 ÷ 12 = $3172.50 $\approx$ $3170.00 per month

17. 4 1/2" + 3 1/4" + 7 1/2" = 15 1/4" = 1 ft. 3 1/4 in.

18. 9 ft. 3 in. = 9 1/4 ft., 6 ft. 9 in. = 6 3/4 ft. Area = (9 1/4) (6 3/4) = 62 7/16 sq.ft.

19. A cubic yard = (3)(3)(3) = 27 cubic feet

20. (450')(.02) = 9 ft.

21. 6/4 = 1 1/2 revolutions

22. Station 42 + 51
    30 ft away would be 51 + 30 = 81 OR 51 - 30 = 21
    Station 42 + 81 or 42 + 21 (ANSWER: B)

23. 30 miles in 60 minutes means 10 miles in 20 minutes.

24. There are 2000 pounds in a ton.

25. ($45.00)(.60) = $27.00 savings per day. For 45 days, his savings is (45)($27.00) = $1215.00

———

READING COMPREHENSION
UNDERSTANDING AND INTERPRETING WRITTEN MATERIAL
EXAMINATION SECTION
TEST 1

DIRECTIONS: Each question or incomplete statement is followed by several suggested answers or completions. Select the one that BEST answers the question or completes the statement. *PRINT THE LETTER OF THE CORRECT ANSWER IN THE SPACE AT THE RIGHT.*

Questions 1-3.

DIRECTIONS: Questions 1 through 3, inclusive, are to be answered in accordance with the following paragraph.

All cement work contracts, more or less, in setting. The contraction in concrete walls and other structures causes fine cracks to develop at regular intervals. The tendency to contract increases in direct proportion to the quantity of cement in the concrete. A rich mixture will contract more than a lean mixture. A concrete wall which has been made of a very lean mixture and which has been built by filling only about one foot in depth of concrete in the form each day will frequently require close inspection to reveal the cracks.

1. According to the above paragraph,   1._____

    A.   shrinkage seldom occurs in concrete
    B.   shrinkage occurs only in certain types of concrete
    C.   by placing concrete at regular intervals, shrinkage may be avoided
    D.   it is impossible to prevent shrinkage

2. According to the above paragraph, the one of the factors which reduces shrinkage in   2._____
    concrete is the

    A.   volume of concrete in wall
    B.   height of each day's pour
    C.   length of wall
    D.   length and height of wall

3. According to the above paragraph, a rich mixture   3._____

    A.   pours the easiest
    B.   shows the largest amount of cracks
    C.   is low in cement content
    D.   need not be inspected since cracks are few

Questions 4-6.

DIRECTIONS: Questions 4 through 6, inclusive, are to be answered SOLELY on the basis of the following paragraph.

It is best to avoid surface water on freshly poured concrete in the first place. However, when there is a very small amount present, the recommended procedure is to allow it to evaporate before finishing. If there is considerable water, it is removed with a broom, belt, float, or by other convenient means. It is never good practice to sprinkle dry cement, or a mixture of cement and fine aggregate, on concrete to take up surface water. Such fine materials form a layer on the surface that is likely to dust or hair check when the concrete hardens.

4. The MAIN subject of the above passage is

    A. surface cracking of concrete
    B. evaporation of water from freshly poured concrete
    C. removing surface water from concrete
    D. final adjustments of ingredients in the concrete mix

4.___

5. According to the above passage, the sprinkling of dry cement on the surface of a concrete mix would MOST LIKELY

    A. prevent the mix from setting
    B. cause discoloration on the surface of the concrete
    C. cause the coarse aggregate to settle out too quickly
    D. cause powdering and small cracks on the surface of the concrete

5.___

6. According to the above passage, the thing to do when considerable surface water is present on the freshly poured concrete is to

    A. dump the concrete back into the mixer and drain the water
    B. allow the water to evaporate before finishing
    C. remove the water with a broom, belt, or float
    D. add more fine aggregate but not cement

6.___

Questions 7-9.

DIRECTIONS: Questions 7 through 9, inclusive, are to be answered ONLY in accordance with the information given in the paragraph below.

Before placing the concrete, check that the forms are rigid and well braced and place the concrete within 45 minutes after mixing it. Fill the forms to the top with the wearing-course concrete. Level off the surfaces with a strieboard. When the concrete becomes stiff but still workable (in a few hours), finish the surface with a wood float. This fills the hollows and compacts the concrete and produces a smooth but gritty finish. For a non-gritty and smoother surface (but one that is more slippery when wet), follow up with a steel trowel after the water sheen from the wood-troweling starts to disappear. If you wish, slant the tread forward a fraction of an inch so that it will shed rain water.

7. Slanting the tread a fraction of an inch gives a surface that will

    A. have added strength
    B. not be slippery when wet
    C. shed rain water
    D. not have hollows

7.___

8. In addition to giving a smooth but gritty finish, the use of a wood float will tend to   8._____

    A. give a finish that is slippery when wet
    B. compact the concrete
    C. give a better wearing course
    D. provide hollows to retain rain water

9. Which one of the following statements is most nearly correct?   9._____

    A. Having checked the forms, one may place the concrete immediately after mixing same.
    B. One must wait at least 15 minutes after mixing the concrete before it may be placed in the forms.
    C. A gritty compact finish and one which is more slippery when wet will result with the use of a wood float.
    D. A steel trowel used promptly after a wood float will tend to give a non-gritty smooth finish.

Questions 10-11.

DIRECTIONS: Questions 10 and 11 are to be answered SOLELY on the basis of information contained in the following paragraph.

Tools and plastering methods have changed very little over the years. Most of the changes are mere improvements of the basic tools. The tools formerly made by hand are now machine-made and are *rigidly* constructed of light, but strong, materials in contrast to the clumsy constructions of the early types. The power-driven mixers and hoisting equipment used on large plastering jobs today produce better mortars and lighten the tasks involved.

10. According to the above paragraph, present day tools used for plastering   10._____

    A. have made plastering much more complicated than it used to be
    B. are heavier than the old-fashioned tools they replaced
    C. produce poorer results but speed up the job
    D. are lighter and stronger than the hand-made tools of the past

11. As used in the above paragraph, the word *rigidly* means MOST NEARLY   11._____

    A. feeble   B. weakly   C. firmly   D. flexibly

Questions 12-18.

DIRECTIONS: Questions 12 through 18 are to be answered in accordance with the following paragraphs.

SURFACE RENEWING OVERLAYS

A surface renewing overlay should consist of material which can be constructed in very thin layers. The material must fill surface voids and provide an impervious skid-resistant surface. It must also be sufficiently resistant to traffic abrasion to provide an economical service life.

Materials meeting these requirements are:
    a.   Asphalt concrete having small particle size
    b.   Hot sand asphalts
    c.   Surface seal coats

Fine-graded asphalt concrete or hot sand asphalt can be constructed in layers as thin as one-half inch and fulfill all requirements for surface renewing overlays. They are recommended for thin resurfacing of pavements having high traffic volumes, as their service lives are relatively long when constructed properly. They can be used for minor leveling, they are quiet riding, and their appearance is exceptionally pleasing. Seal coats or slurry seals may fulfill surface requirements for low traffic pavements.

12.   A surface renewing overlay must fill surface voids, provide an impervious skid-resistant surface, and   12.___

    A.   be resistant to traffic abrasion
    B.   have small particle size
    C.   be exceptionally pleasing in appearance
    D.   be constructed in half-inch layers

13.   An *impervious skid-resistant surface* means a surface that is   13.___

    A.   rough to the touch and fixed firmly in place
    B.   waterproof and provides good gripping for tires
    C.   not damaged by skidding vehicles
    D.   smooth to the touch and quiet riding

14.   The number of types of materials that can be constructed in very thin layers and are also suitable for surface renewing overlays is   14.___

    A. 1   B. 2   C. 3   D. 4

15.   The SMALLEST thickness of asphalt concrete or hot sand asphalt that can fulfill all requirements for surface renewing overlays is _____ inch(es).   15.___

    A. ¼   B. ½   C. 1   D. 2

16.   The materials that are recommended for thin resurfacing of pavements having high traffic volumes are   16.___

    A.   those that have relatively long service lives
    B.   asphalt concretes with maximum particle size
    C.   surface seal coats
    D.   slurry seals with voids

17.   Fine-graded asphalt concrete and hot sand asphalt are quiet riding and are also   17.___

    A.   recommended for low traffic pavements
    B.   used as slurry seal coats
    C.   suitable for major leveling
    D.   exceptionally pleasing in appearance

18. The materials that may fulfill surface requirements for low traffic pavements are   18._____

    A. fine-graded asphalt concretes
    B. hot sand asphalts
    C. seal coats or slurry seals
    D. those that can be used for minor leveling

Questions 19-25.

DIRECTIONS: Questions 19 through 25 are to be answered SOLELY on the basis of the paragraphs below.

OPEN-END WRENCHES

Solid, non-adjustable wrenches with openings in one or both ends are called open-end wrenches. Wrenches with small openings are usually shorter than wrenches with large openings. This proportions the lever advantage of the wrench to the bolt or stud and helps prevent wrench breakage or damage to the bolt or stud.

Open-end wrenches may have their jaws parallel to the handle or at angles anywhere up to 90 degrees. The average angle is 15 degrees. This angular displacement variation permits selection of a wrench suited for places where there is room to make only a part of a complete turn of a nut or bolt. Handles are usually straight, but may be curved. Those with curved handles are called S-wrenches. Other open-end wrenches may have offset handles. This allows the head to reach nut or bolt heads that are sunk below the surface.

There are a few basic rules that you should keep in mind when using wrenches. They are:

    I.   ALWAYS use a wrench that fits the nut properly. Otherwise, the wrench may slip, or the nut may be damaged.
    II. Keep wrenches clean and free from oil. Otherwise, they may slip, resulting in possible serious injury to you or damage to the work.
    III. Do NOT increase the leverage of a wrench by placing a pipe over the handle. Increased leverage may damage the wrench or the work.

19. Open-end wrenches   19._____

    A. are adjustable
    B. are solid
    C. always have openings at both ends
    D. are always S-shaped

20. Wrench proportions are such that wrenches with _____ openings have _____ handles.   20._____

    A. larger; shorter   B. smaller; longer
    C. larger; longer   D. smaller; thicker

21. The average angle between the jaws and the handle of a wrench is _____ degrees.   21._____

    A. 0   B. 15   C. 22   D. 90

22. Offset handles are intended for use MAINLY with

    A. offset nuts
    B. bolts having fine threads
    C. nuts sunk below the surface
    D. bolts that permit limited swing

23. The wrench which is selected should fit the nut properly because this

    A. prevents distorting the wrench
    B. insures use of all wrench sizes
    C. avoids damaging the nut
    D. overstresses the bolt

24. Oil on wrenches is

    A. *good* because it prevents rust
    B. *good* because it permits easier turning
    C. *bad* because the wrench may slip off the nut
    D. *bad* because the oil may spoil the work

25. Extending the handle of a wrench by slipping a piece of pipe over it is considered

    A. *good* because it insures a tight nut
    B. *good* because less effort is needed to loosen a nut
    C. *bad* because the wrench may be damaged
    D. *bad* because the amount of tightening can not be controlled

22.____
23.____
24.____
25.____

KEY (CORRECT ANSWERS)

1.	D		11.	C
2.	B		12.	A
3.	B		13.	B
4.	C		14.	C
5.	D		15.	B
6.	C		16.	A
7.	C		17.	D
8.	B		18.	C
9.	A		19.	B
10.	D		20.	C

21.	B
22.	C
23.	C
24.	C
25.	C

TEST 2

DIRECTIONS: Each question or incomplete statement is followed by several suggested answers or completions. Select the one that BEST answers the question or completes the statement. *PRINT THE LETTER OF THE CORRECT ANSWER IN THE SPACE AT THE RIGHT.*

Questions 1-3.

DIRECTIONS: Questions 1 through 3 are to be answered SOLELY on the basis of the following passage.

A utility plan is a floor plan which shows the layout of a heating, electrical, plumbing, or other utility system. Utility plans are used primarily by the persons reponsible for the utilities, but they are important to the craftsman as well. Most utility installations require the leaving of openings in walls, floors, and roofs for the admission or installation of utility features. The craftsman who is, for example, pouring a concrete foundation wall must study the utility plans to determine the number, sizes, and locations of the openings he must leave for piping, electric lines, and the like.

1. The one of the following items of information which is LEAST likely to be provided by a utility plan is the

   A. location of the joists and frame members around stairwells
   B. location of the hot water supply and return piping
   C. location of light fixtures
   D. number of openings in the floor for radiators

   1.____

2. According to the passage, the persons who will *most likely* have the GREATEST need for the information included in a utility plan of a building are those who

   A. maintain and repair the heating system
   B. clean the premises
   C. paint housing exteriors
   D. advertise property for sale

   2.____

3. According to the passage, a repair crew member should find it MOST helpful to consult a utility plan when information is needed about the

   A. thickness of all doors in the structure
   B. number of electrical outlets located throughout the structure
   C. dimensions of each window in the structure
   D. length of a roof rafter

   3.____

Questions 4-9.

DIRECTIONS: Questions 4 through 9 are to be answered SOLELY on the basis of the following passage.

The basic hand-operated hoisting device is the tackle or purchase, consisting of a line called a fall, reeved through one or more blocks. To hoist a load of given size, you must set up a rig with a safe working load equal to or in excess of the load to be hoisted. In order to do this, you must be able to calculate the safe working load of a single part of line of given size, the safe working load of a given purchase which contains a line of given size, and the minimum size of hooks or shackles which you must use in a given type of purchase to hoist a given load. You must also be able to calculate the thrust which a given load will exert on a gin pole or a set of shears inclined at a given angle, the safe working load which a spar of a given size used as a gin pole or as one of a set of shears will sustain, and the stress which a given load will set up in the back guy of a gin pole or in the back guy of a set of shears inclined at a given angle.

4. The above passage refers to the lifting of loads by means of   4.___

    A. erected scaffolds   B. manual rigging devices
    C. power-driven equipment   D. conveyor belts

5. It can be concluded from the above passage that a set of shears serves to   5.___

    A. absorb the force and stress of the working load
    B. operate the tackle
    C. contain the working load
    D. compute the safe working load

6. According to the above passage, a spar can be used for a   6.___

    A. back guy   B. block   C. fall   D. gin pole

7. According to the above passage, the rule that a user of hand-operated tackle MUST follow is to make sure that the safe working load is AT LEAST   7.___

    A. equal to the weight of the given load
    B. twice the combined weight of the block and falls
    C. one-half the weight of the given load
    D. twice the weight of the given load

8. According to the above passage, the two parts that make up a tackle are   8.___

    A. back guys and gin poles   B. blocks and falls
    C. rigs and shears   D. spars and shackles

9. According to the above passage, in order to determine whether it is safe to hoist a particular load, you MUST   9.___

    A. use the maximum size hooks
    B. time the speed to bring a given load to a desired place
    C. calculate the forces exerted on various types of rigs
    D. repeatedly lift and lower various loads

Questions 10-15.

DIRECTIONS: Questions 10 through 15 are to be answered SOLELY on the basis of the following set of instructions.

PATCHING SIMPLE CRACKS IN A BUILT-UP ROOF

If there is a visible crack in built-up roofing, the repair is simple and straightforward:

1. With a brush, clean all loose gravel and dust out of the crack, and clean three or four inches around all sides of it.
2. With a trowel or putty knife, fill the crack with asphalt cement and then spread a layer of asphalt cement about 1/8 inch thick over the cleaned area.
3. Place a strip of roofing felt big enough to cover the crack into the wet cement and press it down firmly.
4. Spread a second layer of cement over the strip of felt and well past its edges.
5. Brush gravel back over the patch.

10. According to the above passage, in order to patch simple cracks in a built-up roof, it is necessary to use a   10._____

    A. putty knife and a drill   B. knife and pliers
    C. tack hammer and a punch   D. brush and a trowel

11. According to the above passage, the size of the area that should be clear of loose gravel and dust before the asphalt cement is first applied should   11._____

    A. be the exact size of the crack itself
    B. extend three or four inches on all sides of the crack
    C. be 1/8 inch greater than the size of the crack itself
    D. extend the length of the roofing strip

12. According to the above passage, loose gravel and dust in the crack should be removed with a   12._____

    A. brush   B. felt pad   C. trowel   D. dust mop

13. Assume that both layers of asphalt cement needed to patch the crack are of the same thickness.   13._____
The total thickness of asphalt cement used in the patch should be MOST NEARLY _____ inch.

    A. 1/2   B. 1/3   C. 1/4   D. 1/8

14. According to the instructions in the above passage, how large should the strip of roofing felt be cut?   14._____

    A. Three of four inches square
    B. Smaller than the crack and small enough to be surrounded by cement on all sides of the strip
    C. Exactly the same size and shape of the area covered by the wet cement
    D. Large enough to completely cover the crack

15. The final or finishing action to be taken in patching a simple crack in a built-up roof is to   15._____

    A. clean out the inside of the crack
    B. spread a layer of asphalt a second time
    C. cover the crack with roofing felt
    D. cover the patch of roofing felt and cement with gravel

Questions 16-17.

DIRECTIONS: Questions 16 and 17 are to be answered SOLELY on the basis of the information given in the following paragraph.

Supplies are to be ordered from the stockroom once a week. The standard requisition
form, Form SP21, is to be used for ordering all supplies. The form is prepared in triplicate,
one white original and two green copies. The white and one green copy are sent to the stockroom, and the remaining green copy is to be kept by the orderer until the supplies are
received.

16. According to the above paragraph, there is a limit on the 16.___

    A. amount of supplies that may be ordered
    B. day on which supplies may be ordered
    C. different kinds of supplies that may be ordered
    D. number of times supplies may be ordered in one year

17. According to the above paragraph, when the standard requisition form for supplies is pre- 17.___
pared,

    A. a total of four requisition blanks is used
    B. a white form is the original
    C. each copy is printed in two colors
    D. one copy is kept by the stock clerk

Questions 18-21.

DIRECTION: Questions 18 through 21 are to be answered SOLELY on the basis of the following passage.

The Oil Pollution Act for U. S. waters defines an *oily mixture* as 100 parts or more of oil in
one million parts of mixture. This mixture is not allowed to be discharged into the prohibited
zone. The prohibited zone may, in special cases, be extended 100 miles out to sea but, in
general, remains at 50 miles offshore. The United States Coast Guard must be contacted to
report all *oily mixture* spills. The Federal Water Pollution Control Act provides for a fine of
$10,000 for failure to notify the United States Coast Guard. An employer may take action
against an employee if the employee causes an *oily mixture* spill. The law holds your
employer responsible for either cleaning up or paying for the removal of the oil spillage.

18. According to the Oil Pollution Act, an *oily mixture* is defined as one in which there are 18.___
_____ parts or more of oil in _____ parts of mixture.

    A. 50; 10,000   B. 100; 10,000
    C. 100; 1,000,000   D. 10,000; 1,000,000

19. Failure to notify the proper authorities of an *oily mixture* spill is punishable by a fine. Such 19.___
fine is provided for by the

    A. United States Coast Guard
    B. Federal Water Pollution Control Act
    C. Oil Pollution Act
    D. United States Department of Environmental Protection

20. According to the law, the one responsible for the removal of an *oily mixture* spilled into   20.____
    U.S. waters is the

    A. employer
    B. employee
    C. U.S. Coast Guard
    D. U.S. Pollution Control Board

21. The *prohibited zone,* in general, is the body of water   21.____

    A. within 50 miles offshore
    B. beyond 100 miles offshore
    C. within 10,000 yards of the coastline
    D. beyond 10,000 yards from the coastline

Questions 22-25.

DIRECTIONS: Questions 22 through 25 are to be answered SOLELY on the basis of the fol-
               lowing paragraph.

Synthetic detergents are materials produced from petroleum products or from animal or
vegetable oils and fats. One of their advantages is the fact that they can be made to meet a
particular cleaning problem by altering the foaming, wetting, and emulsifying properties of a
cleaner. They are added to commonly used cleaning materials such as solvents, water, and
alkalies to improve their cleaning performance. The adequate wetting of the surface to be
cleaned is paramount in good cleaning performance. Because of the relatively high surface
tension of water, it has poor wetting ability, unless its surface tension is decreased by addition
of a detergent or soap. This allows water to flow into crevices and around small particles of
soil, thus loosening them.

22. According to the above paragraph, synthetic detergents are made from all of the follow-   22.____
    ing EXCEPT

    A. petroleum products   B. vegetable oils
    C. surface tension oils   D. animal fats

23. According to the above paragraph, water's poor wetting ability is related to   23.____

    A. its low surface tension
    B. its high surface tension
    C. its vegetable oil content
    D. the amount of dirt on the surface to be cleaned

24. According to the above paragraph, synthetic detergents are added to all of the following   24.____
    EXCEPT

    A. alkalines   B. water   C. acids   D. solvents

25. According to the above paragraph, altering a property of a cleaner can give an advantage in meeting a certain cleaning problem.
The one of the following that is NOT a property altered by synthetic detergents is the cleaner's

   A. flow ability   B. foaming property
   C. emulsifying property   D. wetting ability

25.___

KEY (CORRECT ANSWERS)

1.	A	11.	B
2.	A	12.	A
3.	B	13.	C
4.	B	14.	D
5.	A	15.	D
6.	D	16.	D
7.	A	17.	B
8.	B	18.	C
9.	C	19.	B
10.	D	20.	A

21.	A
22.	C
23.	B
24.	C
25.	A

THE ENGLISH AND METRIC SYSTEMS OF MEASUREMENT

TABLE OF CONTENTS

THE ENGLISH AND METRIC SYSTEMS OF MEASUREMENT

A. The English System. Tables of weights and measures have been established by law and custom. These units of measurement are concrete numbers commonly referred to as *denominate numbers.*

1. LINEAR (LINE OR LONG) MEASURE

Used in measuring distances and lengths, widths, or thicknesses.

12 inches (in.)	= 1 foot (ft.)
3 feet	= 1 yard (yd.)
5 1/2 yards, or 16 1/2 feet	= 1 rod (rd.)
40 rods	= 1 furlong (fur.).
8 furlongs, or 320 rods	= 1 mile (mi.)

The unit of length is the yard.
1 hand = 4 inches (used in measuring the height of horses).
1 fathom (marine measure) = 6 feet (used in measuring depths at sea).
1 knot = 1.152 1/2 miles (nautical or geographical mile).
1 league = 3 knots (3 X 1.15 miles).

2. SQUARE (SURFACE) MEASURE

Used in measuring areas of surfaces.

144 square inches (sq. in.)	= 1 square foot (sq. ft.)
9 square feet	= 1 square yard (sq. yd.)
30 1/4 square yards	= 1 square rod (sq. rd.)
160 square rods	= 1 acre (A.)
640 acres	= 1 square mile (sq. mi.)

The unit in measuring land is the acre, except for city lots.
A square, used in roofing, is 100 square feet.
The unit in measuring other surfaces is the square yard.

3. CUBIC MEASURE

Used in measuring the volume of a body or a solid as well as the contents or capacity of hollow bodies.

1,728 cubic inches (cu. in.)	= 1 cubic foot (cu. ft.)
27 cubic feet	= 1 cubic yard (cu. yd.)
231 cubic inches	= 1 gallon (gal.)
24 3/4 cubic feet	= 1 perch (P.)
128 cubic feet	= 1 cord (cd.)
1 cubic foot	= 7 1/2 gallons

1 cubic yard of earth = 1 load.
A cord of wood (128 cubic feet) is a pile 8 feet long, 4 feet wide, and 4 feet high.
1 cubic foot of water weighs 62 1/2 pounds (avoirdupois).

4. CIRCULAR OR ANGULAR MEASURE

Used in measuring angles or areas of circles.

60 seconds (")	= 1 minute (')	30 degrees = 1 sign (1/12 of a circle)	
60 minutes	= 1 degree (°)	60 degrees = 1 sextant (1/6 of a circle)	
360 degrees	= 1 circle (cir.)	90 degrees = 1 quadrant (1/4 of a circle)	

A 90° angle is a right angle.

5. LIQUID MEASURE

Used in measuring the liquid capacity of vessels or containers of all liquids except medicine.

4 gills (gi.)	= 1 pint (pt.)	63 gallons	= 1 hogshead (hhd.)
2 pints	= 1 quart (qt.)	2 barrels	= 1 hogshead
4 quarts	= 1 gallon (gal.)	7 1/2 gallons	= 1 cubic foot
31 1/2 gallons	= 1 barrel (bbl.)		

The unit of liquid measure is the United States gallon of 231 cubic inches.
1 gallon of water weighs 8 1/3 pounds (avoirdupois).

6. DRY MEASURE

Used in measuring the volume of the contents of containers of solids, such as produce, seed, fruits, etc., that are not sold by weight.

2 pints (pt.)	= 1 quart (qt.)	4 pecks = 1 bushel (bu.)	
8 quarts	= 1 peck (pk.)	2 3/4 bushels = 1 barrel	

7. AVOIRDUPOIS WEIGHT

Used in weighing heavy, coarse articles, such as coal, iron, grain, hay, etc.

16 ounces (oz.)	= 1 pound (lb.)
100 pounds	= 1 hundredweight (cwt.)
20 hundredweights	= 1 ton (T.)
2,000 pounds	= 1 ton
2,240 pounds	= 1 long or gross ton
7,000 grains (gr.)	= 1 pound avoirdupois

The United States Government uses the long ton of 2,240 pounds in fixing the duty on merchandise that is taxed by the ton.
Coal and iron sold at the mine are also weighed by the long ton.

8. TROY WEIGHT

Used in weighing precious minerals, and by the United States Government in weighing coins.

24 grains	= 1 pennyweight (pwt.)
20 pennyweights	= 1 ounce
12 ounces	= 1 pound
240 pennyweights	= 1 pound
5,760 grains	= 1 pound troy
3,168 grains	= 1 carat

The unit of weight in the United States is the troy pound.

Pure gold is 24 carats fine. Gold marked 14 carats is 14/24, by weight, pure gold and 10/24, by weight, alloy.

9. APOTHECARIES' DRY WEIGHT AND LIQUID MEASURE

Used by druggists and physicians in weighing and measuring drugs and chemicals, and in compounding dry and liquid medicines.

APOTHECARIES' DRY WEIGHT

20 grains	= 1 scruple (sc.)
3 scruples	= 1 dram (dr.)
8 drams	= 1 ounce (oz.)
12 ounces	= 1 pound (lb.)

APOTHECARIES' FLUID MEASURE

60 minims (m.)	= 1 fluid drachm, or dram (f3)
8 fluid drachms	= 1 fluid ounce (f3)
16 fluid ounces	= 1 pint (O.)
8 pints	= 1 gallon (Cong.)

Avoirdupois weight is used when drugs and chemicals are bought and sold wholesale.

10. TIME TABLE

60 seconds (sec.)	= 1 minute (min.)	52 weeks	= 1 year (yr.)
60 minutes	= 1 hour (hr.)	12 months	= 1 year
24 hours	= 1 day (da.)	365 days	= 1 year*
7 days	=1 week (wk.)	100 years	= 1 century (C.)
30 days	=1 month (mo.)*		

* January, 31 days; February, 28 days (29 days in February in a leap year of 366 days); March, 31 days; April, 30 days; May, 31 days; June, 30 days; July, 31 days; August, 31 days; September, 30 days; October, 31 days; November, 30 days; December, 31 days.

11. COUNTING TABLE

20 units	= 1 score
12 units	= 1 dozen
12 dozen	= 1 gross (gro.)
12 gross	= 1 great gross (gr. gro.)

12. PAPER MEASURE

24	sheets	= 1 quire (qr.)
20	quires	= 1 ream (rm.)
2	reams	= 1 bundle (bdl.)
5	bundles	= 1 bale (bl.)

13. MEASURES OF VALUE

United States Money

10 mills	= 1 cent
10 cents	= 1 dime
10 dimes	= 1 dollar
10 dollars	= 1 eagle

The unit of measure is the dollar.

English Money

4	farthings (far.)	= 1 penny (d)
12	pence	= 1 shilling (s.)
20	shillings	= 1 pound sterling ()

The unit of measure is the pound sterling.

French Money

10 millimes (m.)	= 1 centime (c.)
10 centimes	= 1 decime (dc.)
10 decimes	= 1 franc (F.)

The unit of measure is the franc.

German Money

100 pfennig (pf.) = 1 mark

The unit of measure is the mark.

14. COMMODITY WEIGHTS

Beef, barrel	200	lbs.	Nails, keg	100	lbs.
Butter, firkin	56	lbs.	Pork, barrel	200	lbs.
Flour, barrel	196	lbs.	Salt, barrel	280	lbs.

15. BUSHEL WEIGHTS

The following weights are used in a bushel in most of the states:

Barley	48 lbs.	Corn (shelled)	56 lbs.	Potatoes	60 lbs.
Beans	60 lbs.	Corn meal	48 lbs.	Rye	56 lbs.
Buckwheat	48 lbs.	Oats	32 lbs.	Sweet potatoes	54 lbs.
Clover seed	60 lbs.	Onions	57 lbs.	Timothy seed	45 lbs.
Corn (ear)	70 lbs.	Peas	60 lbs.	Wheat	60 lbs.

B. The Metric System. The metric system of weights and measures is a decimal system. The three principal units are
1. The meter, which is the unit of length.
2. The liter, which is the unit of capacity.
3. The gram, which is the unit of weight or mass.

The basic unit of the metric system is the meter, upon which the other units are based. The length of the meter, which is 39.37 inches, was originally determined by taking one ten-millionth of the distance from the equator to the pole.

I. METRIC TABLES
1. LINEAR MEASURE

10 millimeters (mm.)	= 1 centimeter (cm.)
10 centimeters	= 1 decimeter (dm.)
10 decimeters	= 1 meter (m.)
10 meters	= 1 decameter (Dm.)
10 decameters	= 1 hectometer (Hm.)
10 hectometers	= 1 kilometer (Km.)
10 kilometers	= 1 myriameter (Mm.)

The unit of measures of length is the meter.

2. SQUARE MEASURE

100 square millimeters (sq. mm.)	= 1 square centimeter (sq. cm.)
100 square centimeters	= 1 square decimeter (sq. dm.)
100 square decimeters	= 1 square meter (sq. m.)
100 square meters	= 1 square decameter (sq. Dm.)
100 square decameters	= 1 square hectometer (sq. Hm.)
100 square hectometers	= 1 square kilometer (sq. Km.)

The unit of square measures is the square meter.

3. CUBIC MEASURE

1,000 cubic millimeters (cu. mm.)	= 1 cubic centimeter (cu. cm.)
1,000 cubic centimeters	= 1 cubic decimeter (cu. dm.)
1,000 cubic decimeters	= 1 cubic meter (cu. m.)
1,000 cubic meters	= 1 cubic decameter (cu. Dm.)
1,000 cubic decameters	= 1 cubic hectometer (cu. Hm.)
1,000 cubic hectometers	= 1 cubic kilometer (cu. Km.)

The unit of measures of volume is the cubic meter.

4. LIQUID AND DRY MEASURE

10 milliliters (ml.)	= 1 centiliter (cl.)	10 liters	= 1 decaliter (Dl.)
10 centiliters	= 1 deciliter (dl.)	10 decaliters	= 1 hectoliter (Hl.)
10 deciliters	= 1 liter (1.)	10 hectoliters	= 1 kiloliter (Kl)

The unit of capacity for liquids and solids is the liter.

5. WEIGHT TABLE

10 milligrams (mg.)	= 1 centigram (eg.)
10 centigrams	= 1 decigram (dg.)
10 decigrams	= 1 gram (g.)
10 grams	= 1 decagram (Dg.)
10 decagrams	= 1 hectogram (Hg.)
10 hectograms	= 1 kilogram (Kg.)
10 kilograms	= 1 myriagram (Mg.)
10 myriagrams	= 1 quintal (Q.)
10 quintals	= 1 tonneau (T.)

The unit of weight is the gram.

II. METRIC AND ENGLISH EQUIVALENTS
1. LINEAR-MEASURE EQUIVALENTS

1 in. = 2.54 cm.	1 cm. = .3937 in.
1 ft. = .3048 m.	1 dm. = .328 ft.
1 yd. = .9144 m.	1m. = 1.0936 yds.
1 rd. = 5.029 m.	1 Dm. = 1.9884 rds.
1 mi. = 1,6093 Km.	1Km. = .6214 mi.

2. SQUARE-MEASURE EQUIVALENTS

1 sq. in. = 6.452 sq. cm.	1 sq. cm. = .155 sq. in.
1 sq. ft. = .0929 sq. m.	1 sq. dm. = .1076 sq.ft.
1 sq. yd. = .8361 sq. m.	1 sq. m. = 1.196 sq. yds.
1 sq. rd. = 25.293 sq. m.	1 a. = 3.954 sq. rds.
1A. = 40.47 a. (ares)	1 ha. = 2.471 A.
1 sq. mi. = 259 ha. (hectares	1 sq. Km. = .3861 sq. mi.

3. CUBIC-MEASURE EQUIVALENTS

1 cu. in. = 16.387 cu. cm.	1 cu. cm. = .061 cu. in.
1 cu. ft. = 28.317 cu. dm.	1 cu. dm. = .0353 cu. ft.
1 cu. yd. = .7646 cu. m.	1 cu. m. = 1.308 cu. yds.
1 cd. = 3.624 st. (steres)	1 st. = .2759 cd.

4. LIQUID- AND DRY-MEASURE EQUIVALENTS

1 dry qt. = 1.1011.	1l. = .908 dry qt.
1 liquid qt. = .94631.	1l. = 1.0567 liquid qt.
1 liquid gal. = .3785 Di.	1Dl. = 2.6417 liquid gal.
1 pk. .881 Dl.	1Dl. = 1.135 pk.
1 bu. .3524 Hl.	1Hl. = 2.8377 bu.

5. WEIGHT-MEASURE EQUIVALENTS

1 qt. Troy = .0648 g.	1 g. = 15.432 gr. Troy
1 oz. Troy = 31. 104 g.	1 g. = .03215 oz. Troy
1 oz. Avoir. = 28.35 g.	1 g. = .03527 oz. Avoir.
1 lb. Troy = .3732 kg.	1 kg. = 2.679 lbs. Troy
1 lb. Avoir. = .4536 kg.	1 kg. = 2.2046 lbs. Avoir.
1 T. (short) = .9072 1.	1 t. = 1.1023 T. (short)

III. *THE RELATIONSHIP OF AMERICAN AND METRIC UNITS*

Pounds (avoirdupois)	X	.454	= Kilograms
Pounds (avoirdupois)	X	453.592	= Grams
Grams	X	.035	= Ounces
Ounces	X	28.35	= Grams
Kilograms	X	2.205	= Pounds
Grams	X	.002205	= Pounds
Quarts (liquid)	X	.946	= Liters
Quarts (liquid)	X	946.333	= Milliliters
Liters	X	1.057	= Quarts
Liters	X	1000.	= Milliliters
Milliliters	X	.001057	= Quarts